No

Daily Reflections for Lent 2008

Angela Ashwin

LITURGICAL PRESS
Collegeville, Minnesota

www.litpress.org

1   2   3   4   5   6   7   8

ISSN: 1550-803X

ISBN-13: 978-0-8146-2990-1
ISBN-10: 0-8146-2990-3

Introduction

Lent is a good time to adopt the simple daily discipline of taking a moment to be quiet and reflect on Scripture passages from the *Lectionary for Mass* for this season. The meditations in this book are designed to help this process, not in the sense of offering a definitive interpretation of any particular passage, but to prompt the reader to open up heart and mind to the creative activity of the Holy Spirit.

In our journey through Lent we are invited to turn and return continuously to our God whose essential nature is self-giving love. As we ponder the infinite cost of the divine love for us, seen in the passion of Jesus, we have an opportunity to rededicate our lives to the love and service of God and of our neighbor (see Mark 12:30-31).

My prayer is that those who share this journey of reflection through Lent will find encouragement and a deepening of love and commitment to Christ, who freely accepted death for us.

Return!

Readings: Joel 2:12-18; 2 Cor 5:20–6:2; Matt 6:1-6, 16-18

Scripture:
Even now, says the LORD,
return to me with your whole heart,
with fasting, and weeping, and mourning;
Rend your hearts, not your garments,
and return to the LORD, *your God.* (Joel 2:12-13)

Reflection: As we enter the challenge and commitment of Lent, our penitence and prayer will meet the infinite mercy of God. A powerful word in today's reading from the prophet Joel is "return." By returning and turning our faces back towards God, we can find a way through guilt into forgiveness and hope, rather than staying in the dead end of self-reproach and despair. Our returning to God is not to be a mediocre or half-hearted gesture, but will require our "whole heart," a willingness to open ourselves up in complete trust as we expose our deepest being to God.

Facing up to our weaknesses and confessing our sins is always a rigorous business if we do it honestly. In Hebrew thought the "heart" is the center and source of all our motives and desires, so we are challenged to "rend [our] hearts, not [our] garments" in a radical process of self-examination. Yet we do not make our confessions out of fear or dread, as if we had to plead with an angry God in order to make God love us. Mercy is pure gift, unearned and undeserved; it is the result of God's generous initiative towards us, seen supremely in Jesus, whose whole life confirms Joel's insight that God is "slow to anger" and "rich in kindness" (2:13), longing to cleanse, heal, and transform us.

Conversion, which means, literally, "turning around," is an ongoing process and not a once-only event, since we all need constantly to turn back to God—and this present moment is all we have. "Even *now*," says Joel (v.12; emphasis mine), God is calling us. In today's second reading, Paul echoes this urgency in his words, "*now* is a very acceptable time . . . *now* is the day of salvation" (2 Cor 6:2; emphasis mine). This is a clarion call to turn back to the divine wellspring of abundant mercy. Let us not miss the moment.

Meditation: Am I so preoccupied and distracted by superficial things that I forget to turn my heart and soul back to God?

Prayer: Merciful God, grant me the grace to return to you wholeheartedly, and to acknowledge the ways in which I have fallen short.

Choose Life!

Readings: Deut 30:15-20; Luke 9:22-25

Scripture: *I have set before you life and death, the blessing and the curse. Choose life, then, that you and your descendants may live, by loving the LORD, your God, heeding his voice, and holding fast to him.* (Deut 30:19-20)

Reflection: These words of God, originally addressed to the Israelites coming out of Egypt towards the Promised Land, challenge us to be true to our best and wisest selves, and to walk in the ways of integrity and faithfulness. Like the children of Israel, we are confronted with a choice. We can love and serve God and discover life in all its fullness, or we can turn away from God's goodness and face the consequences. Thus we will find ourselves facing either "life" or "curse" (see Deut 30:19).

The Israelites grumbled because life in the wilderness was so harsh that they wanted to go back to slavery in Egypt. We too may be tempted by the comparative security of our particular bondage, such as an overdependence on possessions, or the need for approval at any cost. The process by which God frees us from these things may be costly, but it will ultimately bring us a deeper sense of peace and wholeness.

In the Gospel for today Jesus develops this teaching, saying that those who try to save their own life will lose it, while those who are prepared to lose their life for his sake will save it (see Luke 9:24). The clue to this paradox lies in the question that follows: "What profit is there for one to gain the whole world yet lose or forfeit himself?" (v. 25).

Our God is the loving Creator who desires what is life-giving for us, not what is death dealing. If we cling to the false values of prestige and power, or give in to negative attitudes such as resentment or jealousy, we may lose touch with our very selves. But the grace of God comes to our help when we turn back once more to the divine mercy, and surrender ourselves into the loving presence of the God who will cleanse and remake us.

Meditation: What are the attachments that pull me away from my better self? What do I most want, deep down?

Prayer: O God, help me to lose myself daily in you, that I may become more truly the person you created me to be, in your image.

The Motive Is Love

Readings: Isa 58:1-9a; Matt 9:14-15

Scripture: *Can the wedding guests mourn as long as the bridegroom is with them? The days will come when the bridegroom is taken away from them, and then they will fast.* (Matt 9:15)

Reflection: The disciples of John the Baptist cannot understand why Jesus and his followers have not been observing the usual fasts. Jesus' response shows that we can easily fast for the wrong reasons. He knows that the Pharisees love to show off their virtue and self-control when they fast (see Matt 6:5), hoping to earn God's favor by keeping the letter of the law. Jesus, however, is a free spirit and knows that it is not appropriate for his disciples to be fasting while he is with them. Yet he does not dismiss fasting altogether—indeed, he himself had fasted during his forty days in the wilderness, when he was wrestling with his vocation as God's "beloved Son" (Matt 3:17; see 4:1-11). What, then, does Jesus consider a good reason to fast?

His answer is clear: the motive is love. To illustrate this, Jesus chooses a startling image, describing himself as a bridegroom. After a marriage ceremony there would be elaborate festivities lasting for days, and it is in these joyful terms that Jesus sees his earthly ministry. At such a time, a rigid adherence to the Pharisees' system of fasting simply would not fit. But the time for fasting will come, says Jesus, when he will be taken away and killed. It is for this reason that many of us do make acts of self-denial on Fridays and in Lent, out of love and sorrow at Jesus' suffering, and in penitence for our sins.

Here Jesus is in tune with the great Old Testament prophets, who insist that mere observance of rules is useless without commitment to God and our neighbor (see Mark 12:30-31).

This, rather, is the fasting that I wish
. . . Sharing your bread with the hungry,
    sheltering the oppressed and the homeless,
Clothing the naked . . . " (Isa 58:6-7).

True fasting involves costly self-giving, not in order to gain merit or prove anything to God, but simply out of generosity and love. And when we do this, something in us is healed: "Then your light shall break forth like the dawn, / and your wound shall quickly be healed" (Isa 58:8).

Meditation: What concrete signs of penitence and generosity can I make this Lent?

Prayer: Purify my heart, O God, that I may act with no ulterior motive but simply out of a desire to love and serve you.

Like a Watered Garden

Readings: Isa 58:9b-14; Luke 5:27-32

Scripture:
He will renew your strength, and you shall be like a watered garden, like a spring whose water never fails. (Isa 58:11)

Reflection: Isaiah tells us that if we do our best to live and act with a spirit of generosity, standing up against injustice and feeding the hungry, we will find ourselves richly blessed:

. . . light shall rise for you in the darkness,
. . . Then the LORD will guide you always. (Isa 58:10-11a)

This passage contains a wonderful assurance of hope. Sometimes we may feel that our response is woefully inadequate, when we become aware of the extent of the dreadful oppression and poverty endured by millions of people. But as long as we go on caring and trying to do what we can, God promises to refresh and strengthen us, watering the parched earth of our hearts and minds with the divine compassion.

Fortunately we are not required to put right all our failures and confusions by our own efforts. What God asks of us is a generous heart because this unblocks the channels of grace, allowing God's gentle Spirit to permeate our lives, making us once more "like a watered garden" (Isa 58:11).

Levi, a tax collector, is someone who found his life filled with wellsprings of joy when he responded with total generosity to Jesus' call (see Luke 5:27). While tax collectors were despised by most people, Jesus clearly saw Levi as a valuable human being, full of potential. When Levi realized that Jesus had chosen him to be his follower and friend, Levi was so overwhelmed with joy that he instantly left everything behind: his job, his home, his possessions, and his credibility in the shady world of financial dealings with the Roman occupiers.

Like Levi, we are loved and affirmed by God so much that we can confidently let go of all that stops us being true to our best selves. When we are generous with our time and resources, the result is blessing and joy. Levi didn't mourn for all that he had given away—he had a party!

Meditation: God offers us the immense privilege of following Christ's way of love and generosity. Even if this is costly, can I say, "Yes"?

Prayer: Teach me, God, to be generous in my attitudes, words and actions; open my heart to the living waters of your guiding presence.

March 5: First Sunday of Lent

Into the Desert

Readings: Gen 9:8-15; 1 Pet 3:18-22; Mark 1:12-15

Scripture: *The Spirit drove Jesus out into the desert, and he remained in the desert for forty days, tempted by Satan . . . and the angels ministered to him.* (Mark 1:12-15)

Reflection: Jesus has just had the shattering experience of being baptized by John in the Jordan and emerging from the water to hear God saying to him, "You are my beloved Son" (Mark 1:11). As a result, Jesus feels compelled to go straight into the desert, so that he can be alone with God and come to terms with the extraordinary implications of his unique relationship with the One he knows as Father.

There is dramatic urgency in this picture of Jesus as he strides without hesitation into the barren waste of the Judean wilderness, a place where he will be shaken to the core by the subtle temptations of the evil one. In the vast emptiness of the desert Jesus will be exposed to all that Satan can throw at him. He will be tempted to abuse his divine sonship in order to gain security, popularity, and worldly power, and will certainly need the support of the angels. It is a sobering thought to ponder what would have happened if Jesus had given in to the subtle whisperings of the enemy.

This story will be echoed in some ways at the end of Jesus' life, in the accounts of his ordeal in the Garden of

Gethsemane (see Luke 22:39-46 and parallels). There, too, he will wrestle with the temptation to abandon the task that he has to fulfill and to put his own desire for comfort first. Again there will be a threefold pattern of prayer, as he returns three times to find the disciples sleeping. Significantly, an angel will minister to him on that occasion too.

But now, at the beginning of his earthly ministry, Jesus is moving into life rather than death, and emerges from the wilderness immensely strong in spirit, ready to proclaim the Good News of God's reign among us, news which is destined to change the world.

Meditation: As followers of Jesus, we too may need times apart in order to wait quietly on God and discern the direction in which our life needs to go. Do I give myself this opportunity?

Prayer: Abba, Father, give me strength to resist all that would spoil or distort the person you have created me to be; stay close when I am going through any kind of wilderness experience.

Loving Our Neighbor

Readings: Lev 19:1-2, 11-18; Matt 25:31-46

Scripture: *You shall love your neighbor as yourself.* (Lev 19:18)

Reflection: From the way in which Jesus lived and taught we can see why he picked out these vital words from Leviticus as one of the two cornerstones on which the Law and the Prophets are based, along with loving the Lord our God with all our heart and soul (see Mark 12:30-31; Deut 6:4-5). This clear commandment to love our neighbor in Leviticus forms a refreshing contrast to the previous chapters in that book, which are full of complex and uncompromising regulations concerning uncleanness and purity.

In this passage, grace and generosity are in the foreground. First we are invited to "be holy" as the Lord our God is holy (Lev 19:2). This is a startling idea, paving the way for the wonderful insight in the Second Letter of Peter that we are invited to share in the very nature of God: "that . . . you may come to share the divine nature" (2 Pet 1:4). The commandments that follow are about honesty, truth and generosity of spirit; we know that we cannot obey these through our own initiative alone, but because we are made in God's image and depend on God's grace. Exhortations about not hating others and not bearing a grudge reach a glorious climax in the now famous words, "Love your neighbor as yourself." This, as Jesus has recognized, is the very essence of holiness (see Mark 12:30-31).

Jesus develops this theme of generosity in his parable of the sheep and the goats in today's Gospel, and he gives the message a new twist. Not only is Jesus close to us when we try to help the needy; he is also *in* the hungry, thirsty, naked, and imprisoned people whom we seek to serve: "just as you did it to one of the least of these who are members of my family, mine, you did to me" (Matt 25:40; NRSV). In other words, any action offered in a genuine spirit of love is permeated with the spirit of Jesus, and he is mysteriously present to us in those people whom we are serving. That is food for prayer—and wonder.

Meditation: Do I allow discouragement or apathy to hold me back from giving practical help to those in need?

Prayer: Holy God, make me holy; live and work through me, that I may reflect your gracious compassion to all, especially the marginalized and forgotten.

Finding the Right Perspective

Readings: Isa 55:10-11; Matt 6:7-15

Scripture:
This is how you are to pray:

> *Our Father in heaven,*
> *hallowed be your name,*
> *your kingdom come,*
> *your will be done . . .* (Matt 6:9-10)

Reflection: People sometimes think that prayer is just a matter of asking God for things. Certainly there is nothing wrong with bringing to God our personal concerns and the needs of the world. Yet sometimes our praying can come alarmingly close to giving God information, issuing God with instructions, trying to change God's mind, or attempting to prove how much "faith" we have as we strive to extract the answers we think we want. These are obviously distortions of what Christian prayer is meant to be, as Jesus makes abundantly clear in today's Gospel.

When we pray, he says, we should begin by focusing not on ourselves but on the awesome holiness of God: "Hallowed be your name"! (Matt 6:9). Approaching God with our requests is far more likely to bear fruit when we have first offered ourselves and our lives unconditionally to God: "your kingdom come, / your will be done" (Matt 6:10).

True prayer is as much what God is doing as what we are doing. This is a liberating insight, because we then realize that our praying does not just depend on us. God is also at work when we pray, even when we don't feel that our prayer is much good; as Jesus reminds us, God our Father knows what we need even before we ask (see Matt 6:8). Our loving Creator can only desire what is good and healing for us. By shifting the emphasis away from our own limited perspective onto the life-giving direction of God's will for all humanity, we can tune in to the wavelength of the kingdom and ask God to bring us into harmony with the creative energy that filled Jesus. In this context it makes total sense to ask God for our "daily bread" (Matt 6:11) and ask to be delivered from evil (see Matt 6:13), telling God all our desires and anxieties, like children turning to a wise and loving parent.

Meditation: Say the Our Father slowly and reflectively, remembering that this prayer is a gift that guides us to the heart of the matter—being centered on God.

Prayer: O God, teach me to pray.

We Already Have a Sign

Readings: Jonah 3:1-10; Luke 11:29-32

Scripture: *This generation is an evil generation; it seeks a sign, but no sign will be given it, except the sign of Jonah.* (Luke 11:29)

Reflection: We humans often wish for signs. When I was a young student, someone at a party discovered that I was a Christian and said, "I'd like to see a miracle to prove that God exists!" I felt woefully inadequate as I tried to explain that the God I believe in is not like that, and I have to admit to a fleeting desire to be able to call on God for a miracle then and there! But Jesus constantly resisted the idea that his miracles were to be used as evidence about his divine nature or to boost his popularity. In the wilderness he had rejected Satan's suggestion that he should charm the world into belief by a spectacular jump off the Temple (see Matt 4:5-7), and after he had healed people he often urged them not to spread the news of this abroad. Finally, at the end of his earthly life, Jesus absolutely refused to perform a miracle for the cynical King Herod (see Luke 23:8).

In today's Gospel the only sign that Jesus is prepared to offer to the crowds is "the sign of Jonah" (Luke 11:29). In other words, the ancient people of Nineveh had recognized Jonah as God's messenger and had repented of their evil ways, whereas many in Jesus' time have neither recognized nor heeded him—even though he is "greater than Jonah" (v. 32).

We still seek signs today, yet we are blind to the fact that the supreme and complete sign of God's work among us has already been given—in Jesus. The challenge for us now is to wake up! The risen and eternal Christ is present and active in our midst, as intent on teaching and guiding us today as he was two thousand years ago. He speaks to us, for example, through Scripture and liturgy, through our great traditions of prayer and spirituality, through the brave prophets of justice and peace in our time, and through the needs and the beauty of the world. But are our eyes and hearts open to him?

Meditation: Do I look for Jesus in spectacular things and miss him in the ordinary?

Prayer: O Christ, help me to trust you, even when there is no obvious sign of your presence.

A Passion for the Possible

Readings: Esth C: 12, 14-16, 23-25; Matt 7:7-12

Scripture: *Ask and it will be given to you; seek and you will find; knock and the door will be opened to you.* (Matt 7:7)

Reflection: This is a difficult passage. We know that God is not to be treated as a convenient supplier of our every wish, like a genie in a bottle whom we can summon to suit ourselves. We also know of tragic situations where people have prayed fervently for an obvious good, like the recovery of a desperately sick child, only to find their hopes dashed. So what *does* Jesus mean when he uses these words?

This teaching invites us to embrace a passion for what is possible. It is about developing an attitude of openness, a sense of expectation that we can do all things in the power of Christ who strengthens us (see Phil 4:13). It is easy to play safe when we pray, hovering cautiously at the edges of trust, hardly daring to ask for much and expecting even less. But I would suggest that Jesus is challenging us to be bold in prayer, especially when we pray, "your kingdom come" (Matt 6:10). If we genuinely ask to be blessed and used in the service of the kingdom, who knows what may happen?

To pray in this way is, of course, a dangerous business. God may take us at our word so that we find ourselves facing more than we had bargained for. It is no small thing to ask for the divine light to enter our lives. Yet, challenging though the prospect may seem, we *will* be transformed, and we will receive abundantly if we ask with all our heart to become like Christ.

Jesus is not telling us to try and extract from God whatever we want. Rather, we are to entrust ourselves and our concerns to God, so that we may be taken up into the divine activity in the world.

Meditation: What do I seek when I pray? Am I prepared to be surprised by what may be the result of my prayer?

Prayer: I thank you, God, that you respond to my cautious knocking on your door with a passion and urgency beyond my imagining.

Judge Not

Readings: Ezek 18:21-28; Matt 5:20-26

Scripture: *But I say to you, whoever is angry with his brother [or sister] will be liable to judgment, and whoever says to his brother [or sister], 'Raqa,' will be answerable to the Sanhedrin.* (Matt 5:22)

Reflection: This is another tough saying of Jesus. We all feel angry at times, and we know that to repress a deep anger can lead to emotional and psychological problems later. Furthermore, Jesus himself was clearly angry when he stormed through the Jerusalem Temple, overturning the tables of the moneychangers (see Mark 11:15-19). Seen in context, this passage is not about denying that we feel angry when we clearly do; these words are rather intended to highlight our tendency to judge, mock, and condemn others. Jesus is challenging the judgmental and destructive attitudes that we can so easily adopt, asking us to acknowledge that there may sometimes be another side to a case when we have a grievance.

Even when somebody has blatantly wronged us, it is good to stand back a little and try to understand why the person behaved in that way. But let there be no misunderstanding: it is *perfectly* acceptable to acknowledge and face our hurt and anger. The trouble comes if we then allow our rage to continue festering inside us—because this can build up into a negative energy that damages us and blocks our capacity for wisdom and forgiveness.

Paul frequently exhorts us to be humble, even suggesting that we should "regard others as more important than" ourselves (Phil 2:3). This is not easy when we are reeling from an insult or feel furious about a cruel or unjust act. It may help us to remember that all people are beloved children of God, that only God knows our hearts, and that we ourselves also fall short in many ways. Otherwise we may run the risk of using words we later regret: to call somebody "Raqa" (Matt 5:22) was an extremely offensive rebuke in Jesus' time.

Meditation: When did I last catch myself nursing a grudge? Or have I been harshly critical about someone, without checking my facts or acknowledging that there were mitigating circumstances?

Prayer: God of truth and compassion, you know my inmost heart and understand all that upsets and angers me. Help me to let go of my anger into your safe keeping, and transform the energy of my emotion into a wise response.

March 11: Saturday of the First Week of Lent

With All Your Heart

Readings: Deut 26:16-19; Matt 5:43-48

Scripture: *This day the* LORD, *your God, commands you to ob-serve these statutes and decrees. Be careful, then, to observe them with all your heart and with all your soul.* (Deut 26:16)

Reflection: This passage wakes us up if we are slipping into careless or half-hearted ways in our Christian life. To experience the joy and peace of living close to God, and to know ourselves truly loved and redeemed, we need to be faithful with our whole heart and soul, not just with a part of ourselves. The wonderful thing is that, when we do offer ourselves to God totally, even with all our failings, we find that God is wholly *for us* (Deut 26:18). We also discover that we are "a people peculiarly his own" consecrated or "sa-cred to the LORD" (Deut 26:19). God forms us into the people we are meant to be, and we are not left on our own.

But we can easily start making excuses which prevent us from being true to our highest aspirations. Our commit-ment to prayer can slip when the pressures of daily life build up; our worthy intention to forgive and be reconciled with someone can be compromised when we succumb to the lure of brooding resentment. Our willingness to share our time and resources with others can be rapidly watered down when many demands come at us from all directions.

Lent is a good opportunity to reflect on the generosity of our God, who "makes his sun rise on the bad and the good and causes rain to fall on the just and the unjust" (Matt 5:45). Since God is such a whole-hearted lover of every person, Jesus says that we too should be whole-hearted, not only in the love of our friends, but also of our enemies (see Matt 5:44). This will be costly, but it will also be life-giving.

Meditation: Pray that the heart-center of your life may be in tune with God. Everything else follows.

Prayer: O God, in every decision of my life, help me to stay in tune with the potential to full and generous humanity that you have placed at the center of my being.

A Breathtaking Experience

Readings: Gen 22:1-2, 9a, 10-13, 15-18; Rom 8:31b-34; Mark 9:2-10

Scripture: *This is my beloved Son. Listen to him.* (Mark 9:7)

Reflection: Awe, wonder, mystery, a profound sense of holiness—all these are present in the account of Jesus transfigured on the mountain before Peter, James, and John. In an attempt to describe the indescribable, Mark tells us that "his clothes became dazzling white" (Mark 9:3), and Moses and Elijah join the scene as eternity intersects with time.

What an astonishing way for those three disciples to learn who Jesus is! He could simply have delivered an academic discourse about his divine nature. Instead they have an overwhelming experience which engages their whole selves, body, mind, and spirit.

First there is the physical action, as they climb the mountain. There follows the stunning visual impact in the sight before them, and the verbal input in the declaration from heaven, "This is my beloved Son" (Mark 9:7). Then come the symbolic elements of the enveloping cloud (reminiscent of the presence of God in a pillar of cloud in the wilderness of the Exodus), and the figures of Moses and Elijah, representing the Law and the Prophets. This experience must have touched Peter, James, and John at every level of their being, from their physical senses to their deepest thoughts.

In our prayer and worship, we too are present to the mystery of God with our whole selves, not just our brains. And, just as God declares Jesus to be his "beloved Son" (Mark 9:7), we, too, can listen to God saying to us, "*You* are my beloved son," "*You* are my beloved daughter."

Jesus had already heard these words "You are my beloved Son" (Mark 1:11) addressed to him directly when he was baptized by John in the Jordan. Through our own baptism we are also God's beloved ones; it is well said that prayer is letting God love us, and hearing God call each of us, "Beloved."

Meditation: Imagine yourself on the mountain with Peter, James and John, and ponder the wonder and beauty of the transfigured Jesus. Hear God say to you, "You are my beloved son" or "my beloved daughter."

Prayer: In stillness and adoration, and in union with Jesus my brother, I receive your love, my God.

Awesome Mercy

Readings: Dan 9:4b-10; Luke 6:36-38

Scripture: *But yours, O Lord, our God, are compassion and forgiveness!* (Dan 9:9)

Reflection: Picture a group of people curled in on themselves, tight and fearful. Then picture them slowly opening out their arms, reaching out confidently to a powerful, healing, cleansing light that is streaming out towards them. Penitential prayer is like that. We reach out to God in trust and openness, expressing sorrow and penitence for our sins. And in today's first reading, Daniel is acting on behalf of the whole people of Israel, as he opens his heart and mind to the justice and mercy of our great God.

There is a profound sense of awe here. God is not to be trifled with, nor God's mercy taken for granted. Yet we need not cringe fearfully either. Like Daniel, we can dare to confess our sins honestly and completely, in the sure trust that God's "merciful covenant" (Dan 9:4) with us will be kept.

Sometimes people almost seem to *want* a punishing God, who will give us the terrible security of the "eye for an eye" kind of justice (Matt 5:38, for example, mentions this). But Jesus repudiates this view of God's ways, and instructs us in today's Gospel to be generous and "Be merciful, just as . . . your Father is merciful" (Luke 6:36). This is not to say that we can be casual about our sins or about the destructive power of evil. The Cross reveals how infinitely costly divine forgiveness is. But mercy and compassion have the last word, both in God's dealings with us and in our attitude to each other, if we are following God's way.

It is all too easy to be judgmental. But Jesus' words are clear: "Stop judging and you will not be judged" (Luke 6:37). Forgiveness is a gift, from God to us, and through us to others. It is not a cheap gift—it is awesome in its source and power.

Meditation: Daniel stood before God on behalf of his people. It is worth remembering that, when we confess our sins, we do it on behalf of the world as well as for ourselves, since we all share responsibility for the injustices and cruelty in the world.

Prayer: Like a flower opening up in the sunlight, I open my heart to you, O God. Forgive my sins and the sins of humanity; show us how to live as you desire.

March 14: Tuesday of the Second Week of Lent

A Positive View of Penitence

Readings: Isa 1:10, 16-20; Matt 23:1-12

Scripture:
Put away your misdeeds from before my eyes;
  cease doing evil; learn to do good. (Isa 1:16-17)

Reflection: True penitence is a positive affair. We are not required to drag ourselves down into a slough of morbid self-hatred and despair. What we need, and what God offers us, is not *dis*couragement, but *en*couragement. If we acknowledge our failings honestly before God, our former negative intentions and energies can, by grace, be transformed into goodness and care for others: "[L]earn to do good. / Make justice your aim: redress the wronged, / hear the orphan's plea, defend the widow" (Isa 1:17).

I have met some people who have been crippled by guilt, unable to accept that their wrongdoing could ever be totally forgiven. But this passage gives us a wonderfully vivid and liberating image. Even though our sinfulness feels like a shameful "scarlet" robe enveloping our heart, God will make us "white as snow" (Isa 1:18). No matter how awful or beyond the pale we believe ourselves to be, God's forgiving love will cleanse and purify us. All that is needed is that we turn back and again engage in a dialogue with God. The invitation comes in some remarkably gentle words, "Come now, let us set things right, / says the LORD" (Isa 1:18) or, as the New Jerusalem Bible translates it, "Come, let us talk this over."

Love never forces us to respond, and we are free to reject God's mercy if we so choose; but we bring all kinds of trouble on ourselves if we do: "if you refuse and resist, / the sword shall consume you" (Isa 1:20). God always holds open for us the opportunity to repent, however many times we have fallen away. Lent is a good time to pause and reflect on the shortcomings not only in our actions but also in our attitudes, for today's teaching applies to all that we do and think and are. We can do this in a spirit of hope and trust in God's transforming power, rather than in despair.

Meditation: Where do I most often fall down in terms of unkindness, resentment, or selfishness? How can I make these things springboards into goodness, kindness, and generosity of spirit?

Prayer: Loving Lord, I give you my sins and weaknesses; show me how, by your grace, to "learn to do good" (Isa 1:17) and transform these things into points of growth.

March 15: Wednesday of the Second Week of Lent

They Are Digging a Pit for Me!

Readings: Jer 18:18-20; Matt 20:17-28

Scripture:
Heed me, O LORD,
and listen to what my adversaries say.
Must good be repaid with evil
that they should dig a pit to take my life? (Jer 18:19-20)

Reflection: Jeremiah's story is dramatic, but his situation is a parable of what can happen to any of us. He is a brave and outspoken prophet, obeying God's call to challenge the idolatry, dishonesty, and corruption of the Judean people in the late seventh and early sixth century B.C.E. His message is predictably unpopular, and his enemies plot against him and have him thrown into a muddy pit.

Most of us are not called to such heroism. But we may find pits being dug for us of a different nature. Perhaps we have tried to stand up for what we believe to be right, only to find ourselves the object of hostility and rejection. At such times we are free to tell God exactly how we feel, as Jeremiah himself often did:

"You duped me, O LORD . . .
. . . I am an object of laughter." (Jer 20:7)

We also know that Jesus, who suffered the ultimate rejection, is alongside us in our pain and will never abandon us.

There is another way in which we can fall into a pit. Suppose we have made a fresh effort to serve God and our neighbors, perhaps in some Lenten commitment. Just when we seem to be doing rather well, we may encounter the pitfall of pride and start thinking that we are more spiritual than other people! Or maybe a surge of old resentment, impatience, or self-pity has surfaced in our minds. When we fall into this sort of pit yet again, we need not wallow in guilt or despair. Instead we can smile at our frailty, pick ourselves up, dust ourselves down, and look into the twinkling eyes of the Christ who stretches out his hand to rescue us and take us further along the way with him.

Meditation: Have other people "dug pits" for me when I have been trying to do the right thing? How have I handled it? And what are the pitfalls I create for myself?

Prayer: Beloved God, I give you my hurts and my failures. Thank you that, whatever is happening to me, I can always turn towards your infinite compassion and grace.

March 16: Thursday of the Second Week of Lent

We Have Received What Is Good

Readings: Jer 17:5-10; Luke 16:19-31

Scripture: *Abraham replied, "My child, remember that you received what was good during your lifetime, while Lazarus received what was bad . . . ."* (Luke 16:25)

Reflection: The rich man in this parable made two mistakes during his lifetime: first he was blind to the fact that he was so richly blessed, and second, he failed to be generous to Lazarus, his fellow human being, who was in acute need at his gate.

Gratitude and generosity—Jesus challenges us about these things too. We need to remember how important it is to be thankful for the bountiful goodness of God, who gives us daily so many beautiful, useful and special things. When we become aware of how good this gift of life is, we are more likely to be generous ourselves.

It can be a helpful Lenten exercise to take particular notice, on a single day, of the blessings that surround us: good and loving people, food, clothes, fresh air, flowers and plants, tools and machines, colors and textures, music, books, works of art, peaceful sleep, delightful places—and so much else. Then it is good to ask ourselves how often we think about the plight of the poor and wretched, both locally and worldwide: those who have no decent homes or clean water, who cannot feed their children, those who are abused, or most vulnerable to industrial pollution and the effects of global warming. All of us who live comfortably have a responsibility, like the rich man in the story, to care and to share.

Jesus' parable contains some vivid imagery about the rich man burning in hell. We too could find ourselves trapped in our own little versions of hell if our attention were directed solely towards our own needs and desires, with never a glance at the desperate plight of our hungry and oppressed brothers and sisters. But when we do manage to be generous, or take action in a prophetic or creative way on behalf of those who have very little, we are given a glimpse of heaven.

Meditation: Give thanks for every good thing in this day—you will find a lot if you keep it up! And think about what you could do as positive action on behalf of the poorest and most unhappy people in our world.

Prayer: God of love and mercy, expand my vision and enlarge my heart.

March 17: Friday of the Second Week of Lent

Rejection and Plotting

Readings: Gen 37:3-4, 12-13a, 17b-28a; Matt 21:33-43, 45-46

Scripture: *Come on, let us kill him . . . .* (Gen 37:20)

Reflection: The momentum against Jesus is building up, as his words and actions offend more and more of the religious establishment. He has become such a challenge to the authority of the chief priests, scribes, and Pharisees that they want to destroy him as soon as they can. Jesus is well aware of their plotting. But he also knows that their destructive intention will not have the last word: "The stone that the builders rejected / has become the cornerstone," he says (Matt 21:42), quoting Psalm 118.

Jesus' ultimate victory over the evil intent of his enemies is prefigured by the story of Joseph in today's Old Testament reading. Out of jealousy and ill-will, Joseph's brothers are also plotting murder, but here, too, God will bring good out of evil. Having been left in a cistern in the desert, Joseph is rescued and taken to Egypt, where he will eventually rise to a position of authority. Through his wisdom and skill he is destined to rescue from starvation both the Egyptians and people of many surrounding nations (including his family) during a time of severe famine. In both cases God works *through* the terrible intentions and actions of humankind to bring unimagined goodness out of it all.

On the cross Jesus triumphed over evil. We could not destroy his love, no matter how much hatred and malice we threw at him. After he had gone through and beyond suffering—and death, he let loose into the world a resurrection energy of healing, life, and hope that would change the course of history for ever.

This can encourage us if we ever find ourselves the object of jealousy or aggression. Christ has walked this road before us, and if we give the situation to God, without reserve, God can transform and transfigure our pain into a place of forgiveness and courage, where, by grace, we can become more human rather than less so.

Meditation: Reflect on any time when you have been subjected to jealousy, unkindness, or hostility. Has this made you less human, trapped in your resentment? Or do you desire to become a more human and loving person through what happened?

Prayer: God of mercy, I hold up my small pains to your great agony on the cross. By your grace, make my suffering into a place of light and hope, both for myself and for others.

Healing of Body, Mind, and Spirit

Readings: 2 Kgs 5:1-15; Luke 4:24-30 (Note: usually these readings would be used on Monday of the Third Week of Lent, but this year the Feast of St. Joseph falls on that day. A decision was made to use these readings instead of the Saturday *Lectionary for Mass* readings in this reflection booklet.)

Scripture: *Go and wash seven times in the Jordan, and your flesh will heal, and you will be clean.* (2 Kgs 5:10)

Reflection: The story of the healing of Naaman, the army commander from Aram who suffered from a chronic skin disease, contains much wisdom and a subtle humor. Naaman has a problem of mind as well as body—he is a proud man! In order to find the humility that he needs if he is to become truly whole, this esteemed and powerful man must face a series of tough decisions

First he has to accept advice from two women, one of whom is a foreign slave: "If only my master would present himself to the prophet in Samaria," she says, "he would cure him of his leprosy" (2 Kgs 5:3). So Naaman swallows his pride and sets out to consult a holy man in a distant country. But things get worse when Naaman arrives in Israel, because the king of Israel is rude and irritable, and the prophet Elisha does not even come out of his front door to meet him. Instead the mighty Naaman is instructed to bathe seven times in the Jordan, something that seems to him both trifling and ridiculous. He had expected Elisha to come out and call upon his God in a spectacular demonstration of divine power that would befit someone of Naaman's status! In another ironic twist, Naaman again has to rely on the wisdom of his servants, who point out that he might as well do something simple, seeing as he would willingly have attempted something extraordinary.

With each decision that he takes Naaman grows in stature. Letting go of his dependence on his dignity and social position, he submits himself to the humbling task of bathing in the river. The final step in his journey towards healing and wholeness comes when he gratefully and graciously returns to Elisha and acknowledges Israel's God as the one true God.

Meditation: Often bodily healing needs to be accompanied by a healing of attitudes or memories. Is there any unresolved tension or "dis-ease" in my heart that may be adversely affecting my physical condition?

Prayer: God of compassion, I open up my whole self to you—my memories, my thoughts, my hurts, my longings. Pour your healing power into my body, mind, and spirit.

The Foolishness of God

Readings: Exod: 20:1-17; 1 Cor 1:22-25: John 2:13-25

Scripture: *For the foolishness of God is wiser than human wisdom . . . .* (1 Cor 1:25)

Reflection: Some people distort Christianity by preaching a Gospel of automatic prosperity for believers, and trying to make faith in Jesus into a guarantee of divine protection from suffering. But we are promised no such thing. Jesus brings us life in all its fullness, certainly, but he also invites us to join him along the way of the Cross. The God whom Jesus reveals to us is the One who suffers with and for us, a God who does not offer us an easy exit from our difficulties, but who gives us the strength to face the challenges and trials that may come our way.

Jesus' utter integrity, and his rejection of all hypocrisy and legalism, meant that his death was inevitable, and the terrible way in which he died was, as Paul observes, shocking to some and folly to others (see 1 Cor 1:18). Throughout his ministry, Jesus had turned worldly standards upside down, rejecting the false securities of status, control, and popularity, and choosing instead a path of humility and suffering. He burned with a passionate love for all people, regardless of rank, wealth, or virtue, and this was scandalous in the eyes of the respectable people of his time. The supreme revelation of God's unconquerable love was the Cross itself—hardly what we would have planned had we been given the task of organizing the Incarnation.

Christian discipleship is a paradox. By opening our hearts to the living presence of Christ within us, we are tapping into a strength that will never fail us. But at the same time we may well end up as "fools on Christ's account" (1 Cor 4:10), scorned for our faith and principles. We are not alone, and the Cross shows us that there is, incredibly, suffering in the heart of God. What seems like madness to the world is the greatest source of our hope and joy (see 1 Cor 1). Paul sums up this mystery beautifully in his startling words, "For the foolishness of God is wiser than human wisdom" (1 Cor 1:25).

Meditation: I gaze at the Cross and ponder the folly and the cost of the divine love.

Prayer: O Christ, what have you not suffered, what have you not endured for me?

A Noble Person

Readings: 2 Sam 7:4-5a, 12-14a, 16; Rom 4:13, 16-18, 22; Matt 1:16, 18-21, 24a

Scripture: *When Joseph awoke, he did as the angel of the Lord had commanded him and took his wife into his home.* (Matt 1:24)

Reflection: We owe a considerable debt of gratitude to Joseph, Mary's husband. Not only did he accept a desperate situation in caring for the pregnant Mary when they were only betrothed; he also played key roles in protecting Mary and Jesus from great danger and in bringing Jesus up.

We have no biblical records about what happened during Jesus' childhood and youth, other than the visit of the family to Jerusalem at the age of twelve (see Luke 2:41-51). But by looking at Jesus' words and attitudes in his later life, we can guess how Joseph may have influenced him in those crucial "hidden" years at home in Nazareth. For example, Jesus' teachings show that he knew and delighted in the natural world, and in ordinary people and situations. We can imagine Joseph taking the young Jesus out into the fields and pointing out "the birds in the sky" and the beautiful "wild flowers [that] grow" (Matt 6:26, 28). It is also likely that Joseph's caring attitude to his neighbors and faithfulness to God helped to form Jesus' deep understanding of his Jewish heritage and his compassion for all.

I once heard a homily about St. Joseph in which we were invited to picture him after his death, coming face to face with God and saying, "Well, he's been a credit to you!" Joseph stands in the honorable tradition of the great father-figures in the Hebrew Scriptures, from Abraham to David, and Jesus was their "son" too. We can only wonder at the wisdom of God in choosing these fallible yet outstanding men in the divine purpose of salvation—and that is not to forget the crucial roles of the mothers too!

Meditation: Reflect on the cost to Joseph of his willingness to accept the task of caring for Mary and Jesus. Have you ever had to do something that you knew would be misunderstood and harshly judged?

Prayer: Thank you, God, for the example and inspiration of your faithful servants through the ages, especially St. Joseph, on whom Jesus and Mary depended so much.

Forgiving Others

Readings: Dan 3:25, 34-43; Matt 18:21-35

Scripture: *His master summoned him and said to him, "You wicked servant! I forgave you your entire debt because you begged me to. Should you not have had pity on your fellow servant, as I had pity on you?"* (Matt 18:32-33)

Reflection: It can be hard to forgive, especially if a person has already hurt you a great deal and continues to be unkind or unpleasant. As soon as you think you have worked through one painful incident, something else seems to happen, and old wounds open once more. Wrongly applied, today's Gospel could become a cause for despair for anyone struggling to forgive, or feeling guilty about the way a hurtful individual can bring out the worst in them. A lady with a very demanding elderly relative once said to me, "I hate myself for resenting her, but she is really impossible, and *so* unkind."

In spite of appearances, today's Gospel is *not* telling us that God will automatically have problems forgiving us when we are having difficulty forgiving someone else. God's forgiveness is always there for us if we will only turn and receive it. Jesus has made this clear in many parables, such as the those of "The Lost (Prodigal) Son" (Luke 15:11-32) and "The Good Shepherd" (Luke 15:1-7). Today's parable concerning the unforgiving servant is a warning about those who *deliberately* nurse bitterness and feed on the desire for revenge regardless of any mitigating circumstances. For them, to forgive others would go against the grain and feel like weakness, but that is an attitude that can cut us off from the healing and merciful energy of God. We are all forgiven much, and we need to be merciful people ourselves.

If we ourselves are being hurt by a person whom we are struggling to forgive, we can take heart. Our desire—our very *wanting*—to be able to forgive is what matters most. God sees our hearts and knows when we are not nursing vengeance for its own sake. When we pray for help in this painful situation, we can be sure that God is close, pouring grace and mercy into our hearts even when it doesn't much feel like it.

Meditation: If you are struggling to forgive someone, know how passionately God is pressing to love, heal, and strengthen you.

Prayer: Merciful God, I open up my hurt and anger to you. I know that you understand totally. Grant me the grace to forgive—I cannot do it by my own strength.

Remember!

Readings: Deut 4:1, 5-9; Matt 5:17-19

Scripture: *However, take care and be earnestly on your guard not to forget the things which your own eyes have seen, nor let them slip from your memory as long as you live . . . .* (Deut 4:9)

Reflection: The Jewish faith has a strong tradition of remembering. The Israelites in the Old Testament were often exhorted not to forget that God had brought them out of Egypt and had given them a unique set of "statutes and decrees" that would be the envy of the surrounding nations (see Deut 4:6). This kind of remembering was far more than just recalling facts. In the Hebrew Scriptures "remembering" meant entering afresh into something from the past so that it was brought to life again in present experience. At each celebration of the Passover, the events of the Exodus were recalled and revisited, passed on to "children" and "children's children" in a living tradition (Deut 4:9). Jesus himself developed this rich concept of corporate remembering, taking it to a new and sublime level at the Last Supper when he instructed us to take bread and wine "in *remembrance* of" him (1 Cor 11:24; emphasis mine; cf. Luke 22:19).

Remembering can mean, literally, "re-membering," putting together again that which is broken or divided.

When we remember what God has done for us, we, in our fragmented state, are healed and "re-membered," put together again in some way. This creative remembering can happen in a variety of ways. For example, St. Ignatius often recommends that we recall and re-engage with moments in prayer in which we had grown spiritually or been particularly inspired. This can be especially helpful if we are going through a tough time. The purpose is not to try and recreate a past experience for its own sake. It is rather to open up again an area in which the Holy Spirit had been moving in us, so that God can work in us even more deeply now.

Meditation: Look back over your faith journey of the past years. Note down any events, encounters, or places which helped you to grow spiritually. Choose one that seems to draw your attention now, and revisit it with thankfulness. Stay with this in your prayer, open your heart to God, and see what happens.

Prayer: O God, help me to remember the moments and insights that you want me to cherish and keep alive in my heart.

March 23: Thursday of the Third Week of Lent

Divided or Unified?

Readings: Jer 7:23-28; Luke 11:14-23

Scripture: *Every kingdom divided against itself will be laid waste and house will fall against house.* (Luke 11:17)

Reflection: We now know that there are chemical or external causes behind most mental illnesses, and that, with a *very* few exceptions, such conditions are not due to possession by the devil or evil spirits, as was believed in New Testament times. But we can still see how the power of evil can cause havoc in us, both as individuals and in humanity as a whole.

Jesus makes a sharp response to those who suggest that he has cast out demons by the prince of demons, pointing out that he would be divided against himself if that were the case. This reminds us how easily we can be divided against ourselves. Most of us experience times when our surface desires are in conflict with our better selves. Maybe a part of us very much wants something that we know, deep down, would harm ourselves or other people. Perhaps the temptation to gossip or be greedy or be unfaithful is getting the better of us. Many such things can fragment us, so that we desperately need Christ to "re-member" us (as we saw yesterday), and to unify us from the deepest center of ourselves.

The alternative is despair, as the demon of discouragement tempts us to give up trying to live by the best and highest that we know. It is true that we often cannot "pull ourselves together" by our own efforts alone. But the gift of grace is there, whenever we turn to God and cry out in our need and confusion. Then we discover that what holds us together is not our achievements or apparent holiness, but the simple act of acknowledging our need of God, as God's beloved children, cherished, forgiven, and refashioned by God into becoming more the persons we were created to be.

Meditation: What divides me against myself?

Prayer: Strong and gentle God, I am here before you, with all the contradictions of my heart and mind. Help me to be present to you with my whole self. Unify me, and help me, by your grace and mercy, to reconnect with my true self.

Gentle as Dew

Readings: Hos 14:2-10; Mark 12:28-34

Scripture:
"I will be like the dew for Israel:
  he shall blossom like the lily;
He shall strike root like the Lebanon cedar,
  and put forth his shoots." (Hos 14:6-7)

Reflection: What a contrast to the picture of an angry God that appears fairly often in the older Scriptures! All the prophets frequently warn the Israelites that they have brought disaster upon themselves because they have sinned and turned away from goodness and faithfulness to God. But here Hosea balances that stern teaching with a message of hope and restoration. The imagery is extraordinary: our mighty and awesome God will fall "like the dew" on Israel (Hos 14:6)—and upon us too, when we, in our turn, return to God and confess our sins in a true spirit of penitence.

Dew is silent and infinitely gentle; it forms in secret, hidden in the darkness of the night, and sparkles in the morning light in exquisite droplets on cobwebs and blades of grass. *That* is how our God comes to us! We can only wonder at the intimacy and beauty of this image and of the mystery to which it points.

God's anger at our sin and disobedience is only half the story: "I will heal their defection," says the Lord, "I will love them freely; / for my wrath is turned away from them" (Hos 14:5). As Christians we easily become hooked on guilt, rather than seeing penitence as a springboard into the delight and beauty of God's care for us. Hosea teaches that God desires to win us back whenever we have wandered away, just as Hosea himself goes into the wilderness to woo back his unfaithful wife (see Hos 2:14-20).

If you want the dew of divine mercy to fall on your own inner landscape, so that you, too, can "blossom like the lily" (Hos 14:6), it may help if you spend some of your prayer time staying still and quiet, like a garden at night.

Meditation: Set aside five or ten minutes simply for being quiet and open to the secret coming of God into your inmost being.

Prayer: O God, come into my heart like dew and gentle rain on parched earth.

March 25: The Annunciation of the Lord

The Greatness of God

Readings: Isa 7:10-14; Heb 10:4-10; Luke 1:26-38

Scripture: *Hail, full of grace! The Lord is with you.* (Luke 1:28)

Reflection: This account of the Annunciation of the Lord and of Mary's generous response is full of joy. The angel Gabriel's very first greeting, "Hail!" is a word that can also be translated "Rejoice!" Gabriel's message then continues to be positive and joyful in tone as he says, "Do not be afraid, Mary, for you have found favor with God. Behold, you will bear a son . . . He will be great . . . [N]othing will be impossible for God" (Luke 1:30-37). In the end, in spite of her understandable qualms and anxieties, Mary's final "Yes" has the resonance of a total and willing surrender, with no sense of a reluctant giving in to pressure: "Behold, I am the handmaid of the Lord. May it be done to me according to your word" (Luke 1:38).

Mary is overshadowed by the Holy Spirit, and is filled with a mixture of joy and trepidation that we can hardly begin to imagine. This joy will continue beyond this passage, as Mary soon sets out to visit her cousin Elizabeth. In spite of being an old lady, Elizabeth is pregnant with the child John—the one destined to be the Baptist. Luke records Mary's ecstatic outpouring of praise when she arrives at Elizabeth's house: "My soul proclaims the greatness of the Lord!" (Luke 1:46).

There will, of course, be a huge cost too, and Mary will learn from Simeon in the Jerusalem Temple that a sword must pierce her heart (see Luke 2:35). But for now, at this intense and intimate moment where the angel and Mary are face to face, a divine joy is let loose into the world. The joy that fills Mary will spill over into everything that surrounds her, as she fulfils her extraordinary task, enabling God's Son to dwell among us.

Meditation: The thirteenth-century teacher and mystic, Meister Eckhart, once wrote that the eternal birth must take place in each of us. And Paul prayed that Christians might be "filled with all the fullness of God" (Eph 3:19). Am I prepared to be a "God bearer" in the world now?

Prayer: Behold, Lord, your servant. "May it be done to me according to your word" (Luke 1:38).

You Are God's Handiwork

Readings: 2 Chr 36:14-16, 19-23; Eph 2:4-10; John 3:14-21

Scripture: *For we are his handiwork, created in Christ Jesus for the good works that God has prepared . . . .* (Eph 2:10)

Reflection: In this passage phrases about the richness of God's mercy and grace tumble over each other in a great paean of praise and delight. The climax comes in verse 10, where Paul tells us that we ourselves are God's "handiwork" or "God's work of art" (NJB). We are so often reminded of our sinfulness and unworthiness that it is refreshing to hear that our Creator takes as much delight in fashioning us as a master artisan would take over a cherished piece of work. We were created in God's image with infinite love and skill, and we are constantly mended and remade by that same creative energy of divine love. What is more, God desires to do good things through each of us, since we are created "for the good works that God has prepared" (Eph 2:10).

Everything is gift, from the superb intricacy of our bodies to the complexity of our minds and deep yearnings of our spirit. Salvation is also a gift and never our own doing (see Eph 2:8). Sometimes Christians mistakenly assume that our own actions or intellectual beliefs can earn us salvation. But Paul firmly reminds us that it is *"by grace* [we] have been saved through faith" (Eph 2:8; emphasis mine), not the other way round. God still continues to love us and draw us back, even when we least deserve it and have become "dead in our transgressions" (Eph 2:5), wandering far away from what is good.

Many of us go through times when we lack confidence in ourselves. The pressure always to "succeed" can cause much stress and feelings of inadequacy. But God sees us with different eyes and values us for who we are—as a wise and loving parent perceives each of her or his children. To celebrate the fact that we are precious in God's eyes, God's beloved, God's handiwork, is not pride—it is true faith (see Col 3:12; Eph 2:10).

Meditation: What are the gifts God has given me? What do I love doing? What makes me feel more alive? How do I best serve others?

Prayer: Creator God, I place myself in your hands, like a work of art in the hands of the artist. I trust in your unfailing gift of grace.

No More Weeping or Pain

Readings: Isa 65:17-21; John 4:43-54

Scripture:
Thus says the LORD:
"Lo, I am about to create new heavens
  and a new earth
. . . I will rejoice in Jerusalem
  and exult in my people.
No longer shall the sound of weeping be heard there . . . ."
    (Isa 65:8, 17-19)

Reflection: Some people are afraid to pray because of what they fear God may ask of them. They think that "the will of God" must always be painful, or they assume that God deliberately inflicts suffering on us because it will be somehow good for us. But the reading from Isaiah shows how mistaken such ideas are. Here we see how God desires to restore and make new our earthly life: "No longer shall there be in it / an infant who lives but a few days" (65:20). Disease, terrorism, or natural disasters such as the 2004 Asian *tsunami*—God directly desires none of the misery that these things can cause us.

Of course, some of our troubles are the result of our abuse of human freedom; other catastrophes happen because of the nature of this planet, in a mystery that we do not understand. In a sense, life is always dangerous—we need water and fire, for example, but these things can kill us too. What is clear is that Jesus' whole life and ministry were directed towards reaching out in compassion to ease the pain of anyone ravaged by illness or misfortune of any kind.

Recently there was a tragic scene at a hospital near to my home. A baby had just died, and the chaplain was present with the parents. In a clumsy attempt to comfort the parents this priest said, "It was the will of God." The child's father promptly hit him on the jaw. In his desire to produce an explanation of what had happened, the priest had given them a horrific picture of God. The father's behavior may not have been exemplary, but his theological instincts were right. God does not desire the anguish of human beings or deliberately make terrible things happen to us. Jesus came to share our human pain, not to explain it away, and there is anguish in the heart of God over every person whose life is broken.

Meditation: Think about the way Jesus related to those he met in the Gospels, especially those who were hurting or in need.

Prayer: O God, I hold before you all who suffer. Use me as a channel of your blessing.

Life-giving Water

Readings: Ezek 47:1-9, 12; John 5:1-16

Scripture: *Wherever the river flows, every sort of living creature that can multiply shall live, and there shall be abundant fish, for wherever this water comes the sea shall be made fresh.* (Ezek 47:9)

Reflection: In this wonderful vision, Ezekiel sees water trickling, pouring, and then gushing out of the Jerusalem Temple. It flows with purifying power as it heads eastward into the Dead Sea (which is so salty that it can sustain no life at all). In his vision, Ezekiel sees trees along the river bank that are laden with fruit that have medicinal properties, so that many living creatures can be fed and nourished there (see 47:7, 12). In addition, his vision shows the salt waters of the Dead Sea becoming fresh, enabling fish and other living creatures to thrive there.

This is a vivid parable of what can happen in our spiritual lives if we are prepared to receive the living water of Christ's transforming power permeating and flowing through us. Jesus said to the Samaritan woman, "whoever drinks the water I shall give will never thirst; the water I shall give will become in [that one] a spring of water, welling up to eternal life" (John 4:14).

When we pray we are invited to open ourselves up to the cleansing stream of divine mercy and love, offering those parts of our life that feel barren and lifeless so that God's living water may renew us and make us fruitful, like rain soaking into a parched landscape. Jeremiah says that those who trust God are like trees planted by a stream; their roots are sustained, their leaves remain green, and they continue to bear fruit even in times of drought and extreme heat (see Jer 17:7-8). If we remain rooted in God we can trust that God will never dry up on us, however difficult our circumstances. The ways in which we pray will vary according to our circumstances, but a fundamental rootedness in the love of God is at the heart of all Christian commitment.

Meditation: Which areas in my inner landscape need watering and refreshing?

Prayer: "O God, you are my God— / for you I long! / For you my body yearns; / for you my soul thirsts, / Like a land parched, lifeless, / and without water (Ps 63:1-2).

Jesus Is Too Much for Them

Readings: Isa 49:8-15; John 5:17-30

Scripture: *For this reason they tried all the more to kill him, because he not only broke the sabbath but he also called God his own father, making himself equal to God.* (John 5:18)

Reflection: Jesus is a free spirit. He refuses to be bound by a legalism that values the keeping of the law above human wellbeing. Defying some of the contemporary religious authorities and their rigid demands, Jesus has just healed a sick man on the sabbath, next to the pool at Bethesda (yesterday's Gospel). Now Jesus enrages his enemies even more by speaking openly of his intimate relationship with the God he knows as his "Father" (John 5:17). Those who want to keep God as a remote and inaccessible deity are threatened by such familiarity.

Both aspects of Jesus' challenge to these authorities speak to us too. First there is the issue of sabbath observance. All four Gospel writers give us examples of Jesus healing people, and even gathering grain, on the sabbath (see Mark 2:23, for example). The point of the sabbath is to help us come closer to God and become more whole as human beings, not to impose miserable restrictions just for their own sake ("The sabbath was made for humankind, and not humankind for the sabbath" Mark 2:27; NRSV). It has always been tempting for religious people to mistake the letter of the law for its deeper purpose. In Lent it is good to review and strengthen the disciplines that we try to keep in our life of faith and prayer. But it is also healthy to dig deeper and ask ourselves to what extent these disciplines help us grow spiritually.

Second there are implications for us from the way Jesus refers to God as "Father" (see, for example, Luke 23:46), because we are drawn into this loving relationship, so that we too may become sons and daughters of God and address God as "Abba, Father!" (Gal 4:6). God is still the Holy One, utterly beyond our grasp. Yet, at the same time we can enter a love relationship which is as tender and familiar as that between parent and child.

Meditation: You may find it helpful to use the words "Abba, Father!" as a simple prayer, repeated quietly to yourself, and to allow yourself to be drawn, by the Holy Spirit, into Jesus' own prayer to the Father.

Prayer: "Abba, Father!"

The Lure of Worldly Glory

Readings: Exod 32:7-14; John 5:31-47

Scripture: *How can you believe, when you accept praise from one another and do not seek the praise that comes from the only God?* (John 5:44)

Reflection: This is a challenging saying. Jesus himself never succumbed to the attractions of worldly acclaim, nor did he seek a dazzling reputation, even though Satan tried to offer him all these things in the wilderness (see Matt 4:1-11). Here, in the long discourse that John the Evangelist puts into the mouth of Jesus, the teaching is clear: "I do not accept human praise . . . I came in the name of my Father, but you do not accept me" (5:41-43).

We may try to comfort ourselves by assuming that this passage is only addressed to those of high rank or wealth, fame, or power, such as film stars and politicians who depend a great deal on public opinion. But we all need to ask ourselves how far we are dependent on the praise of others, for we can all fall into the trap of placing our ultimate security in our status and reputation rather than in God.

There may come a time when we are sorely tested, finding ourselves standing up for what we believe to be right and facing unpopularity and rejection as a result. Then it is good to remember that we are not alone. Christ is alongside us in our pain and has entered our human vulnerability to its very depths. Another danger that can beset us is the sin of pride, when we are inclined to look down on others or keep to ourselves any praise that we receive. This is not to say that we should be falsely humble, or deny that we have done something well when we know that we have. We are all entrusted with gifts and talents, and it is good to be affirmed and celebrate these things. Receiving praise graciously and truthfully is part of our integrity. But we also need to pass on the praise to God, the Source of all our gifts. The late Cardinal Basil Hume, archbishop of Westminster, was once asked how he handled praise and acclaim. He replied, "I enjoy it, but I don't inhale!"

Meditation: How do I deal with praise and criticism, and the desire to be liked?

Prayer: O God, help me to be true to myself and to place all my security in you.

March 31: Friday of the Fourth Week of Lent

The Authority of Jesus

Readings: Wis 2:1a, 12-22; John 7:1-2, 10, 25-30

Scripture:
So they tried to arrest him, but no one laid a hand upon him,
  because his hour had not yet come. (John 7:30)

Reflection: Today's Gospel reveals the sheer authority and fearlessness of Jesus, as he enters Jerusalem and preaches openly, to the amazement of the crowds who know that his enemies want to kill him (see John 7:26). In spite of their power and control of the people, the Jewish authorities are powerless to stop Jesus publicly proclaiming his unique intimacy with God his Father: "the one who sent me, whom you do not know, is true. I know him, because I am from him, and he sent me" (John 7:28-29). Jesus' enemies are infuriated by this, but still they cannot seize him (see John 7:30).

Later in this Gospel, the evangelist will make it clear that Jesus goes to his death, not because his enemies have outmaneuvered him, but because he has freely chosen to enter the darkness of pain and death for our sakes: "I lay down my life in order to take it up again. No one takes it from me, but I lay it down on my own" (John 10:17-18). In today's Gospel too, we see that Jesus is in control, even when worldly forces are amassing against him.

But who is Jesus claiming to be? The people of Jerusalem are clearly confused, because they are not sure if he matches their expectations of a hidden Messiah: "Could the authorities have realized that he is the Messiah? But we know where he is from. When the Messiah comes, no one will know where he is from" (John 7:26-27). Ironically, Jesus' true identity *is* hidden from them, and his audience only know his human origin. They are unable to grasp the full truth that he has also come from God.

From the earliest centuries, Christians have wrestled with the mystery of how Jesus can be both fully human and fully divine. Today we can still only approach this question in a spirit of awe and wonder.

Meditation: It has been said that silence surrounds the Incarnation (God becoming human, enfleshed). We can never fully comprehend this mystery, but we can worship and adore.

Prayer: O Christ, I praise and adore you for the generosity and single-mindedness with which you gave yourself for us all (see Phil 2).

April 1: Saturday of the Fourth Week of Lent

God, the Tester of Motive and Thought

Readings: Jer 11:18-20; John 7:40-53

Scripture: *Yet I, like a trusting lamb led to slaughter, had not real-ized that they were hatching plots against me . . . .* (Jer 11:19)

Reflection: Both of today's readings give us a picture of wicked and unscrupulous people scheming to destroy an innocent victim. In the case of Jeremiah, his uncompromis-ing message of judgment has caused such strong opposi-tion that he finds himself as vulnerable as a "lamb led to slaughter" (11:19). In many ways, his story foreshadows that of Jesus himself, but Jeremiah calls down vengeance on his enemies (see 11:20), while Jesus will pray for the for-giveness of the soldiers who crucify him: "Father, forgive them, they know not what they do" (Luke 23:34).

In today's Gospel, the momentum of hostility towards Jesus is steadily increasing, along with disputes among his enemies as to whether or not he can be the Christ. Both readings open up the question of integrity: what *are* the motives and innermost thoughts of these two figures, whose enemies are so busy plotting against them? God, who sees into our hearts, knows the truth, and Jeremiah finds consolation in his trust in YHWH as the "searcher of mind and heart" (11:20). Since God knows our deepest de-sires, Jeremiah believes that God will recognize the purity of his intentions, in contrast to the corrupt and self-seeking purposes of those who feel so threatened by his preaching.

John the Evangelist gives us a wonderful example of courage and integrity in Nicodemus, who takes a considerable risk when he points out to fellow members of the Sanhedrin that they have not given Jesus a proper hearing. He receives only scorn and abuse for this, and thus shares a little, as Jeremiah did, in the experience of rejection that would be the lot of Jesus himself. Would we have been so brave?

Meditation: When I open my heart to God, who sees into our inmost being, what will God see?

Prayer: O God, have mercy on me and remake me as you will (see Luke 18:13).

April 2: Fifth Sunday of Lent

Knowing God

Readings: Jer 31:31-34; Heb 5:7-9; John 12:20-33

Scripture: *No longer will they have need to teach their friends and relatives how to know the LORD. All, from least to greatest, shall know me, says the LORD . . . .* (Jer 31:34)

Reflection: Jeremiah describes a startling shift, from a religion of external forms and observances to a faith where God's precepts are written on the heart and people will truly "know the LORD" (31:34). This new way of relating to God enables humankind to grasp and receive more readily the gift of God's mercy: "I will forgive their evildoing and remember their sin no more" (v. 34b).

The Hebrew verb "to know" conveys far more than simply having factual information about a person or thing. This kind of knowing involves the whole person, body, mind, and spirit, and is the same term that is used for the sexual love between a man and a woman: "The man knew his wife Eve" (Gen 4:1; NJB). So we are invited to enter into an intimate, loving relationship with the God who loves and desires us, and wants to forgive us and restore us into a covenant relationship of promise and trust.

In Psalm 46 we are told "Be still and know that I am God!" (v. 10; NRSV). The word for "know" in this verse is the same as that used by Jeremiah in today's passage; it is significant that *knowing* God is linked in the psalm with the still surrender of trust and prayer. This sort of surrender to God is costly because we have to let go of our surface pre-occupations and plunge into the unknown. It is a kind of dying to self, a letting go of the controls so that the Spirit of God can take possession of us.

In the Gospel Jesus speaks of the seed falling to the ground and dying before it can spring up and bear fruit. This obviously applies to himself, but also challenges us to die to ourselves in order to live for him. Knowing God in the surrender of deep prayer is one way of doing this.

Meditation: Let me become quiet and still, listening to the sounds around me and acknowledging God's loving presence with me.

Prayer: I surrender myself to you O God, body, mind, and spirit. You know me utterly; teach me how to know you, and teach me how to let go into you.

How We Use Scripture

Readings: Dan: 13:41c-62; John 8:1-11

Scripture: *Now in the law, Moses commanded us to stone such women.* (John 8:5)

Reflection: There is much disagreement among Christians about how we should use and interpret the Bible. Some believe that each verse of Scripture is of equal value and to be taken literally. Others see the Bible as an evolving collection of various writings by people who, over a period of a thousand years, sought to understand the nature and will of God. Those of us who adhere to the second approach would say that Scripture is inspired but not infallible; it needs to be interpreted according to its context and cultural setting, and in relation to the whole of the Bible, especially the person and message of Jesus.

Those who challenge Jesus in today's Gospel are not using the Scriptures in the way that Jesus wanted. They are rigidly determined to carry out the exact letter of the law, and have made the mistake of focusing all their attention on a single verse, while ignoring the wider theme of judgment tempered with mercy.

Jesus, however, has an intimate knowledge of the desires and purposes of God his Father, and also of people's hearts. He knows that the Pharisees have forgotten their own capacity for sinfulness and have slipped into a ruthless judgmentalism, using the woman's misery and humiliation for their own ends as they try to trap him. Jesus' response to the woman is clear and merciful: "Neither do I condemn you. Go, and from now on do not sin any more" (v. 11).

When we are wondering what is the best way to approach the Bible, we do well to follow Jesus' approach. He treated the Scriptures of his own day with great reverence: "I have come not to abolish but to fulfill" (Matt 5:17). On the other hand, he also declared certain texts outdated: "You have heard that it was said to your ancestors . . . But I say to you . . . " (Matt 5:21ff.).

Meditation: Would you benefit from doing some study of the nature of the texts in the Bible and how they evolved?

Prayer: Wise and generous God, may your Holy Spirit speak to me and guide me as I study and reflect on the Scriptures.

The Cost of Freedom

Readings: Num 21:4-9; John 8:21-30

Scripture: *But with their patience worn out by the journey, the people complained against God and Moses, "Why have you brought us up from Egypt to die in this desert, where there is no food or water?"* (Num 21:5)

Reflection: When the Israelites had been in the wilderness for a while, the physical hardships they encountered made them wish that they were back in the comparative security of slavery in Egypt (see Num 21:5). For us too it can seem much more comfortable to stay in a limited way of being or in an attitude that stops us being fully human, rather than stepping out into freedom with God and letting go of false securities (see Rom 8:21). Perhaps we are overattached to an outmoded routine, or overdependent on public opinion. Maybe we are enslaved to an old and brooding resentment or need to break free of a situation that damages ourselves and others. It takes faith and courage to step out of such things into freedom with God; we *will* face tough moments when we do so, just as the Israelites found it hard to keep going in the desert. But we can trust in the God who is with us through it all, and who gives us signs of his presence and mercy, like the bronze serpent in this passage.

When Moses raised the bronze serpent as a sign of healing and forgiveness for the people who had been filled with
fear and bitten by snakes, he cannot have guessed that his
action mysteriously foreshadowed the lifting up of Christ
for the salvation of all (see John 8:28 where Jesus says:
"When you lift up the Son of Man, then you will realize that
I AM"). In order to receive the gifts of healing and inner
freedom that are offered to us by God, we may need to pass
through some kind of wilderness experience ourselves, as
we let go of the things that diminish us. This may take a
while—the Israelites were impatient that their wanderings
were lasting so long (see Num 21:4). But God will not be
hurried, and we have to trust.

Meditation: In what areas of my life am I not truly free?
Am I trapped by any false securities, possessions, desires,
or fears?

Prayer: O God, I ask for the grace to perceive the things
that enslave me, for strength to let them go, and for the
courage to step into freedom with you.

The Truth That Sets Us Free

Readings: Dan 3:14-20, 91-92, 95; John 8:31-42

Scripture: *If you remain in my word, you will truly be my disciples, and you will know the truth, and the truth will set you free.* (John 8:31-32)

Reflection: Today's Gospel continues yesterday's theme of freedom. Have you ever known or heard about someone who was so inwardly free that he or she was able to face suffering with a deep strength and calm? I knew one such person in South Africa in the 1970s. He was a Lutheran minister who worked in one of the poorest townships of Johannesburg, and he spoke out fearlessly against the injustices and violence that he had witnessed many times inflicted on the black people in his care. He preached about this regularly and also wrote articles in Christian journals across the world. As a result he was harassed and threatened by security forces, his son was told he could not go to university, his office was ransacked by men with dogs, and he received several death threats.

Inevitably all this took its toll, and his health was not good. Yet, in spite of the cost, there was also a deep serenity about him. He knew he could do no other; he could not live a lie or pretend that all was well when clearly it was not. So he freely accepted what he had to do, knowing full well that there would be a price to pay.

Jesus was also aware of the malicious intentions of his enemies: "I know that you are descendents of Abraham. But you are trying to kill me, because my word has no room among you" (John 8:37).

While we may not be asked to be as heroic as the Lutheran pastor, we may, in small ways, find ourselves challenged to be true to what we believe to be right.

Meditation: Are there any situations in which I am tempted to take an easier path rather than following what I know, deep down, to be right?

Prayer: Lord, free me from fear and help me to trust you enough to be true to myself, and to you.

Your Name

Readings: Gen 17:3-9; John 8:51-59

Scripture: *No longer shall you be called Abram; your name shall be Abraham, for I am making you the father of a host of nations.* (Gen 17:5)

Reflection: In biblical times a person's name was significant. It represented your essence, your very self, and to use someone's name in a disrespectful way was the deepest of insults. That is why Jewish people, to this day, will never utter the sacred name of God, "YHWH," but instead say the name *Adonai,* ("My Lord") for the unutterable God.

For the Israelites a change of name meant a change of destiny. "Abram" means "exalted father," or "one of noble descent." The name "Abraham" retains that sense of greatness, but also echoes the Hebrew *ab hamon,* "father of a multitude." His new name expresses what he is in the process of becoming, the father of a great nation of people who will be in a covenant relationship with God (Gen 17:3).

Jesus himself took people's names seriously. For example, he said to Simon, "you are Peter [literally "a rock"], and on this rock I will build my church" (Matt 16:18, NRSV). Saul the Pharisee, who persecuted the early church, would become Paul the apostle after his mind-blowing conversion experience on the road to Damascus (see Acts 13:9).

God calls each of us by name, as beloved sons and daughters. It may be that we are entering a new phase in our lives, or finding, in some sense, a new identity that could be expressed by another name. At such times it may help to reflect on the verse in Revelation 2 which reads: "To everyone who conquers I will give some of the hidden manna, and I will give a white stone, and on the white stone is written a new name that no one knows except the one who receives it" (v. 17; NRSV). You may like to picture a white stone in your hand—or perhaps literally hold one and see what happens.

Meditation: In the Easter garden Mary Magdalene recognized Jesus when he said her name, "Mary!" (John 20:16). Imagine that you are in that garden, and that Jesus calls you by your name.

Prayer: O God, you have called me by my name. I am yours.

April 7: Friday of the Fifth Week of Lent

Making Mistakes

Readings: Jer 20:10-13; John 10:31-42

Scripture:
All those who were my friends
  are on the watch for any misstep of mine.
"Perhaps he will be trapped; then we can prevail,
  and take our vengeance on him." (Jer 20:10)

Reflection: This picture of hostile people watching out to see if someone puts a step wrong can strike a chord for us too. In our modern world we are quick to find fault or take each other to court, even feeling a perverse kind of pleasure if there is someone to blame. We can also seek to exploit the errors of others for our own ends, especially if a mistake is made by someone with whom we have a fundamental disagreement.

Jeremiah, like Jesus, faced enemies who resented his message and wanted to catch him out; they were ready to jump on any error of fact or misjudgment. In the cases of both Jesus and Jeremiah, their enemies failed. But what are the implications when we ourselves make mistakes? It is particularly hard when those who often seem to be working against us pounce on our mistake, and try to use it to undermine us. Or there may be times when we are feeling sore simply because we got something wrong and have been shown up in front of other people.

Perhaps the best way to deal with our mistakes is to treat them as friends not enemies. Our mistakes are often the best growth points we have, giving us the opportunity to learn from what has happened. None of us is perfect, and if we spent all our time and energy trying to avoid error at all costs we would never launch out into any creative or worthwhile enterprise. Even Jesus' disciples made mistakes about his person and purpose. Take Peter, for example: even though he was close to Jesus, and was the first to realize that he was the Messiah, he still could not understand or accept that the Christ had to suffer, and was strongly rebuked by Jesus for suggesting an easier way (see Mark 8:31-33).

Meditation: What mistakes have I made lately? How do I deal with them in my mind and heart?

Prayer: Lord, help me to grow through my errors, and grant me the grace to be thankful for these opportunities to learn.

April 8: Saturday of the Fifth Week of Lent

A Time to Live and a Time to Die (see Eccl 3:2)

Readings: Ezek 37:21-28; John 11:45-56

Scripture:
So from that day on they planned to kill him.
   So Jesus no longer walked about in public . . . but he left for a region near the desert . . . . (John 11:53-54)

Reflection: In the Gospel of John, Jesus has already spoken of his death, describing himself as the good shepherd who lays down his life for the sheep (see 10:15-18). Yet the time is not yet right for him to die, so he avoids danger for the moment by taking his disciples away from the region around Jerusalem into a safer place, just as he had once walked away from a murderous crowd in Nazareth earlier in his ministry (see Luke 4:28-30). We know very well that Jesus is not escaping suffering out of cowardice, but for now, he needs to be protected.

   This can help us to understand the mysterious way in which people of faith sometimes realize that they have been protected by God in dangerous circumstances. I recently attended a lecture given by a Christian who ministers to a congregation in a highly dangerous and volatile situation in the Middle East. Many of them have been killed or threatened, but they still faithfully worship and care for those in need. The speaker told us that he calls on the angels to protect him every time he gets into his car. He knows that he may be killed at any time, and he accepts this, remaining true to his conviction that he must continue to work there for the present. Sometimes he is advised to move into a safer place until a specific danger has passed; he does this, as it is the sensible thing to do. At other times he says that he knows he has been protected from almost certain death. He is a brave human being indeed.

In the Gospel, Jesus too needs to be protected for the moment. But the time is coming when he will "set his face to go to Jerusalem" (Luke 9:51; NRSV) and sacrifice his life for us.

Meditation: Have you ever sensed that you have been protected form some sort of danger or trouble? Has this affected the way you live and respond to God?

Prayer: May the angels guard and protect me and all those whom I love. Keep us close to you, O God; keep us faithful, generous, and unselfish—to the end.

Greeting Our King

Readings: Mark 11:1-10; Isa 50:4-7; Phil 2:6-11; Mark 14:1–15:47

Scripture:
Hosanna!
  Blessed is he who comes in the name of the Lord!
  Blessed is the kingdom of our father David that is to come!
    (Mark 11:9-10)

Reflection: Jesus is moving towards the end of his earthly ministry, and these final days will be full of irony and paradox. Terrible things will be done to him, yet he is freely laying down his life for us (see John 17:17-18). The soldiers will mock him as "the King of the Jews" (Mark 15:18), yet Jesus truly is our king—though not the sort of monarch the world would expect, as his entry into Jerusalem on a donkey demonstrates (see Zec 9:9).

Suddenly Jesus' followers find themselves swept along into the city, amidst an extraordinary outburst of praise and delight. The crowd probably consists of a mixture of local residents from the outskirts of Jerusalem and fellow travelers with Jesus. They have picked up Jesus' intention and are entering wholeheartedly into a spirit of celebration as they joyously affirm who he is and sing their hosannas.

In this procession, which is such a mixture of exuberance and sorrow, Jesus is performing a profoundly symbolic act. By choosing to ride on a donkey, he shows that he is indeed a king—but on his terms, not ours. He is proclaiming his identity as a servant-king who will win our allegiance by love, not by force. There are ironic parallels here with the way Roman emperors would make their triumphal entry into a newly conquered city. The emperor would ride a great white horse, not an ambling donkey. There would be gorgeous flags and banners, rather than people waving palm branches and spreading their garments on the road. The people would cheer, but out of a spirit of fear and subservience, not with the spontaneous cheering that we see here.

The result of Jesus' particular kind of kingship is that he will, in worldly terms, be utterly vulnerable. No wonder his authority will be such a puzzle to Pontius Pilate on Good Friday (see John 18).

Meditation: Am I prepared to open my heart to Christ and let him be king of my life?

Prayer: Jesus, Lord of the journey, I thank you that you set your face firmly towards Jerusalem (see Luke 9:51, NRSV), with a single eye and pure intention, knowing what was ahead but never turning aside.

Extravagant Love

Readings: Isa 42:1-7; John 12:1-11

Scripture: *Mary took a liter of costly perfumed oil . . . and anointed the feet of Jesus and dried them with her hair; the house was filled with the fragrance of the oil.* (John 12:3)

Reflection: On the surface this seems a shocking incident. Mary of Bethany breaks the normal taboos of respectability by pouring a huge amount of expensive oil over Jesus' feet and drying them with her hair. Normally only prostitutes would let down their hair in public, and such a passionate and sensuous action is bound to cause a stir. But Jesus is perfectly happy to allow her to do this because he sees the deep love and gratitude that have prompted such an extravagant gesture.

The four Gospels contain variant accounts of this incident, but they all include the pious disapproval of those who cannot handle what is clearly an intimate moment, both for Jesus and for the woman. Here it is Judas who remonstrates with Jesus: "Why was this oil not sold for three hundred days' wages and given to the poor?" he asks (John 12:5).

Jesus' response shows that he recognizes not only Mary's integrity but also the powerful symbolism in what she has done. She has prepared his body for burial, for she knows what deadly peril he is in. The action of anointing is also associated with kingship (even though it was usually poured over the head rather than the feet; see 1 Sam 10:1). Throughout his passion, Jesus remains our true king, even as worldly rulers try to destroy him

This incident encourages us to do things for God that may seem extravagant in the eyes of the world. "What a waste!" people say, along with remarks like, "Why not sell your beautiful churches and give to the poor?" But today's passage confirms that it is good to lavish our time, gifts, and imagination on the God who is so generous to us. Of course we must feed the hungry—Jesus is quite clear about this elsewhere. But we need not be afraid to allow generosity and beauty to permeate our worship; for its fragrance will linger in our hearts, just as the aroma of the perfumed oil filled the whole house in Bethany (see John 12:3).

Meditation: Do I allow fear of criticism to hold me back from generosity of any kind?

Prayer: Jesus, beloved friend, show me how to love you with everything I am, everything I have.

April 11: Tuesday of Holy Week

Darkness and Glory

Readings: Isa 49:1-6; John 13:21-33, 36-38

Scripture: *Now is the Son of Man glorified . . . .* (John 13:31)

Reflection: At the Last Supper there is an atmosphere of simplicity and intimacy. Jesus has welcomed his closest friends to the fellowship of a meal, and he has already washed their feet. Now he introduces a startling note of sorrow, as he reveals that one of them will betray him. We can imagine the bewilderment and shock of the other disciples as Jesus identifies Judas, sharing a piece of bread with him as he does so. In Matthew's Gospel, Jesus speaks the haunting words, "woe to that man by whom the Son of Man is betrayed. It would be better for that man if he had never been born" (Matt 26:24). This is surely a lament rather than a condemnation, as Jesus' heart must be breaking for Judas.

Jesus then goes further, as if he is almost sharing the weight of responsibility with Judas. "What you are going to do, do quickly," he says (John 13:27). Jesus alone understands the turmoil inside Judas, and the complex motives that are driving him to betray his Master. In the next twenty-four hours, they will both die—you could say they died together. Meanwhile, we can only guess at the level of anger and dread that the other disciples must be feeling as Judas slips away into the shadows.

At the very moment when the powers of evil and darkness appear to be winning, Jesus turns everything upside down. "Now is the Son of Man glorified," he says (John 13:31). In John's Gospel, Jesus' death on the cross is consistently presented as the moment when God's glory is revealed. We shall need to hang on to this eternal perspective as we continue to travel with Jesus through this week of his passion. The last verse of today's reading gives us a solemn glimpse of the painful events to come, when Jesus says to Peter, "Amen, amen, I say to you, the cock will not crow before you deny me three times" (John 13:38).

Meditation: Only the unconquerable divine love can ever find those of us who are lost, or feel destroyed by what we have done.

Prayer: Lord God, whose compassion reaches beyond the heavens and whose love bears and redeems the evil of this world, have mercy on us all.

The Suffering Servant

Readings: Isa 50:4-9a; Matt 26:14-25

Scripture:
I gave my back to those who beat me,
  my cheeks to those who plucked my beard.
My face I did not shield
  from buffets and spitting. (Isa 50:6)

Reflection: This is one of a series of four poetic passages often referred to as the "Servant Songs" within Isaiah 40–55. These fifteen chapters come from a prophet who is often referred to as Deutero-Isaiah (or Second Isaiah). The author probably lived among the Israelites during their exile in Babylon from around 547–540 B.C.E. Each song presents to us a figure who is open and obedient to God, who suffers badly at the hands of others, and whose case is ultimately vindicated by God and used for the good of all.

We cannot be sure whether the servant figure originally referred to an individual, such as the prophet himself, or to the nation of Israel, suffering in exile—or perhaps both. Not surprisingly, Christians have recognized in these songs a profound insight into the suffering that would be endured by Jesus himself, who:

. . . emptied himself,
taking the form of a slave

. . . and found human in appearance,
he humbled himself,
becoming obedient to death,
    even death on a cross. (Phil 2:7-8)

The Gospel echoes this theme of humiliation and suffering and takes us into the final days of Jesus, as Judas betrays him and the passion begins.

The picture of the obedient, suffering servant is both moving and inspiring. We see one who trusts in God utterly, even when everyone abuses and rejects him. We also see someone faithfully committed to rising "[m]orning after morning" in order to listen to God in prayer (Isa 50:4). We occasionally find saints in our own day who are deeply rooted in God and have this sort of calm integrity and courage, even in the face of persecution. They inspire us, even in our mundane situations, to take a few small steps of courage when necessary, knowing that we are very close to Christ and that we depend totally upon the grace of God to see us through.

Meditation: Let us give thanks for Archbishop Pius Ncube of Bulawayo, Zimbabwe, a brave leader and servant of his flock, prepared to stand up for truth, justice, and goodness, whatever the danger to himself.

Prayer: O God, grant me the grace to be your faithful servant, whatever the cost.

A Note about the Triduum

Lent itself ends with the beginning of the Mass of the Lord's Supper on Holy Thursday. At the evening Mass, the Easter Triduum or "Three Days" begins, continuing through Easter Sunday Evening Prayer. The journey through Lent brings us to the final holy days. We continue our prayerful reflections: through the footwashing and institution of the Eucharist, on to the road to Calvary, and to the quiet of Holy Saturday. Then we enter the glory of Easter.

April 13: Holy Thursday

Uncontainable Love

Readings: Exod 12:1-8, 11-14; 1 Cor 11:23-26; John 13:1-15

Scripture: *If I, therefore, the master and teacher, have washed your feet, you ought to wash one another's feet.* (John 13:14)

Reflection: *In preparation for this evening:* Holy Thursday is sometimes called "Maundy Thursday," after the Latin *mandatum* or "command" given by Jesus to the disciples at the Last Supper, that they should "love one another" (John 13:34). Before giving them this new commandment, Jesus has himself acted out the role of a loving servant in an extraordinary way, by washing their feet.

It is likely that this meal was held in the upper room of the house of Mark the Evangelist, where the apostles would continue to meet after Jesus' ascension (see Acts 1:13; 12:12). We can imagine the bewilderment of the young John Mark, who had probably organized the family servants to be ready with water and towels to welcome the guests, only to find Jesus taking the towel himself and proceeding to wash everyone's feet—normally the task of the lowest slave.

This act is as beautiful as it is shocking. Jesus, their Master and Lord, is kneeling before each one and washing their feet, in a most disconcerting glimpse of the lengths to which the love of God will go, too much for most of us to bear. It is a symbolic action, challenging our pride and ambition, and teaching us how to love. It is a new way of showing us that each person is infinitely valuable in God's eyes. It is an unequivocal statement that we—you and I—are also intended to receive this gift of outpouring love.

In what could be considered a humiliating moment, Jesus reveals the power of his inner freedom. It is not surprising that Peter cannot handle this at first. We can only wonder at such love and humility.

Meditation: The late archbishop of Canterbury, Michael Ramsey, once said in a lecture on John's Gospel, "The glory of God is Jesus washing the disciples' feet."

Prayer: O Christ, free me from all my pride and give me a generous heart.

He Was Despised and Rejected

Readings: Isa 52:13–53:12; Heb 4:14-16; 5:7-9; John 18:1–19:42

Scripture: *Then Pilate took Jesus and had him scourged. And the soldiers wove a crown out of thorns and placed it on his head, and clothed him in a purple cloak, and they came to him and said, "Hail, King of the Jews!" And they struck him repeatedly.* (John 19:1-3)

Reflection: Why such brutality? Why did the Roman soldiers unleash such mocking cruelty upon this gentle, courageous, unarmed man? Wasn't it enough that he had already been scourged—a punishment so ferocious that many persons died under that alone?

I believe it was partly a matter of fear. They couldn't cope with Jesus' sheer integrity and inner freedom; he was too much of a threat. Something in them wanted to bring him down to their level and corrupt him a little, to make it easier for them to handle him. They wanted to make him curse and shout at them, make him hate them. But, of course, they could not; so they hurt him all the more. No wonder Pilate said, "Behold, the man!" (John 19:5) when they brought him out again in front of the crowd; although cruelly abused his spirit was undiminished.

In our age we humans are still capable of acts of appalling barbarism, and it is tempting at times to despair.

But perhaps gazing at the figure of Christ, scourged and vilified, can help us to hang on to love in the midst of hate, and hope in the midst of revenge.

Jesus takes into himself and absorbs all the evil that we, the human race, can throw at him. He also transforms the Cross into a focus and symbol of forgiveness and hope. Evil fails to defeat the divine love on Calvary. We cannot stop Christ from loving us, whatever we do to him.

Just before he dies, Jesus wants to say something very important. Because this needs to be heard, he asks for a drink to moisten his parched throat. Then he utters the words, "It is finished!" (John 19:30). This Greek word for "finished" signifies not loss or defeat, but rather a completion. The task is done! All that the evil one can do is now spent. Love has triumphed. It is accomplished.

Meditation: Jesus shows us that there is suffering in the heart of God. In the most violent and frightening situations, Christ crucified is there.

Prayer: Trembling I stand at the foot of your cross, O Christ, and watch.

April 15: Holy Saturday

A Quiet Waiting

Reflection: Today there is quietness and anticipation in the pause between two momentous days. After the noise and crowds of Good Friday there is a sense of stillness and simplicity about today. Jesus' body has been laid in a tomb and some of the women have noted where this is, so that they can prepare spices with which to anoint his body properly after the sabbath ends this evening (see Luke 23:5-56; Mark 15:47–16:1).

As we now wait and prepare for what is to come, we can give thanks for the courage of Joseph of Arimathea. Since he is a member of the Jewish Council or Sanhedrin he has taken a great risk in approaching Pilate to ask for Jesus' body (see Mark 15:43; John 19:38). Apart from him, it appears to be the women who are doing what Jesus' disciples have largely failed to do. At least they have not deserted him completely. Without the faithfulness of these brave people Jesus' body could have been left on the cross for the ravens to feast on, for this is what happened to most crucified people.

Meanwhile we wait and wonder, holding together the pain of what has just happened with the joy of knowing that Christ has not been destroyed and that the powers of evil and sin have not won. Even in the worst moments of the crucifixion narrative we were in fact given a few glimmers of light. In John's Gospel, Jesus' last cry was not one of defeat but of triumph: "It is finished." (John 19:30). And even the Roman centurion on duty that day recognized that Jesus was "the Son of God!" (Mark 15:39).

Meditation: It is good to allow ourselves a chance to be quiet and ponder the events that have happened this week.

Prayer: How quiet, O Christ, is the garden where they placed you in the tomb. Quiet my heart, as I keep vigil for you.

Life-Changing Moments

Readings: Acts 10:34a, 37-43; 1 Cor 5:6b-8; John 20:1-9

Scripture: *[The other disciple] saw and believed. For they did not yet understand the scripture that he had to rise from the dead.* (John 20:8-9)

Reflection: In today's Gospel we see three characters whose lives will be changed irrevocably because of the events that are now unfolding.

First we see Mary Magdalene, who has come to anoint Jesus' body and finds that the stone has been moved from the tomb. We can hear the anguish in her voice as she tells Peter and the beloved disciple, "They have taken the Lord from the tomb, and we don't know where they put him" (John 20:2). She stands there weeping, grief-stricken at the loss of the one who had loved and believed in her. Now it seemed that the opportunity to pay her last respects to Jesus has been taken away. Yet, in the next few moments, Mary will hear Jesus call her by her name (see John 20:16), and she will be overwhelmed with joy and relief.

Then we see Simon Peter, rushing straight into the tomb with typical impetuosity. He must still be devastated that he denied he even knew Jesus, that terrible night in the high priest's courtyard (see John 18:15-17, 25-27). Yet soon he will have a crucial encounter with Jesus by the Sea of Galilee.

Just as he had denied Jesus three times, so Jesus will ask him three times, "Do you love me?" (John 21:15-19), thus offering Peter the deep healing and knowledge of forgiveness that he so desperately needs.

Finally the disciple whom Jesus loved, John, a calmer and more cautious figure, lingers outside the tomb before following Peter inside. More perceptive than the other disciples, this man will be the first to recognize Jesus standing on the shore when they have all gone out fishing (see John 21:7). In John's Gospel we are told that he "saw and believed" (John 20:8)—simply from seeing the linen cloths in the tomb. For the writer of John's Gospel, the testimony of the beloved disciple is central, and the whole purpose of this Gospel is that we who read it "may . . . believe that Jesus is the Messiah . . . [and] may have life" (John 20:31).

Meditation: Picture the risen Jesus here with you now. What would you like to say to him?

Prayer: Risen Lord, I believe!

P46   St. Peter's, ~~Rome~~
       Oratory
       Sister Ellen Mary
       Alanon
       Julie + Seija

A CONVERSATION
WITH JESUS

ON

DOUBT

A CONVERSATION
WITH JESUS
ON

DOUBT

DAVID HELM

CHRISTIAN
FOCUS

Copyright © Holy Trinity Church, Chicago

ISBN 978-1-5271-0328-3

Published in 2019

by

Christian Focus Publications Ltd.,
Geanies House, Fearn, Ross-shire,
IV20 1TW, Great Britain

www.christianfocus.com

Cover design and typeset by: Pete Barnsley (CreativeHoot.com)

Printed in China

CONTENTS

TWO WORDS
BEFORE
BEGINNING

ONE

The book in your hands is one of six. Short volumes all. Think of them as people to meet, not pages to be read. In each, a charcoal sketch is drawn of a person who first appeared on the pages of John's Gospel. Both women and men. Real flesh and blood. All worthy of attention. And each one fully capable of standing on their own two feet.

Beyond this, they all have someone in common. Jesus. The Nazarene. The Christ— he who forever changed the world we live in. Anyway, they all met him. In person. And they talked with him. More than that. Each one had a *conversation with Jesus* about something important to them.

TWO

I suppose something should be said about why 'these six'? Let's just say the selection is subjective. Author's prerogative. I liked them. I wanted to know them. And I learned significant things from each one of them. There are good reasons to think that you will connect with them too. Their struggles are our struggles. Their questions too. In fact, some people are saying there has never been another century to resemble the one these six lived in, until ours came along. And if that is the case, you may just run into yourself by running into them.

At any rate, there came a day when they all ran into Jesus. Of course, he is the only character to emerge in every encounter. I am confident that you will enjoy getting to know him.

DIRECTOR'S
NOTES

CAST:

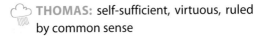

THOMAS: self-sufficient, virtuous, ruled by common sense

JESUS: an educator, ready to move on, bloodied but not bowed

SETTING:

A living room. At night. Sparsely furnished. A few cushions for sitting and a small table or two (with candles on them for light). The door to the outside world is closed, noticeably locked from the inside. A curtain drapes the only window.

A group of young men are sitting, talking and praying in groups of two or three. To one side, though, stands a young man (comfortable in his own skin) in heated discussion with a few of the others.

A CONVERSATION
WITH JESUS ON
DOUBT —

'I have doubted, and still doubt, everything,' replied Levin in a voice unpleasant to himself, and stopped. The priest paused a few seconds to see if Levin would say anything more, and then closing his eyes said rapidly, with a strong provincial accent: 'Doubts are natural to human weakness, but we must pray that our merciful Lord will strengthen us. What are your particular sins?' he continued without the slightest pause, as if anxious not to waste time. 'My chief sin is doubt. I doubt everything and am in doubt nearly all the time.' 'Doubt is natural to human weakness,' repeated the priest. 'What do you doubt in particular?' 'Everything. Sometimes, I even doubt the existence of God,' said Levin involuntarily, and was horrified at the impropriety of his words. But they seemed to have no effect on the priest.

—ANNA KARENINA[1]

Doubt is a virtue. An asset. A needed check on blind certainty. Without it, that is, without some measure of reservation on most things, we would *certainly* end up making a mess of everything.

THE BENEFITS OF DOUBT

Can you imagine what would become of us if doubt was pushed aside and ruled out of bounds? For one thing, entire fields of inquiry would be threatened. Meaningful questions in the pursuit of knowledge would be quashed. The freedom to disagree openly and honestly with the conclusions of others would be wrecked. The study of philosophy, scientific experimentation, and the ability to challenge established traditions would be silenced. Take away 'reasonable doubt,' and you shut down more than our court systems, you call down the entire human enterprise. And at what cost? At the cost of the joyful discovery of something new? Of arriving at a more complete understanding of our world and the way it works? At the cost of losing the chance of improving things for everyone? In other words, at the cost of *real* things, better things, things that can be proven, trusted, and rationally called true. Yes, doubt is a virtue. An asset. And not merely as a check on blind certainty; doubt stimulates us to pursue a nobler world.

I suppose this accounts for our appreciation of people who embody the best of doubt. Women and men who 'think things through before giving themselves to…,' whether that be to something or someone. We are right to admire individuals who live with their eyes wide open. In this short book, we are going to meet one such person. He has famously been named *Doubting Thomas*. And we can meet him in the Gospel of John.[2]

The sketch we can draw of Thomas from the Bible is fascinating. First, he was one of Jesus' early hand-picked followers. That is to say, there was something distinctive about him.

Jesus wanted Thomas to be with him. And by selecting him, other individuals, perhaps less forceful in expressing variant opinions, must have been passed by. From what I can make of out of Thomas (he appears three times in conversation with Jesus in John's Gospel), he is someone who commands respect. He comes off as an unflinchingly loyal insurrectionist, a no-nonsense conversationalist, and a scientifically-minded empiricist. To put it another way, he was a man who challenged accepted norms, stated his own mind on a matter, and required reasonable evidence before adopting a position. And more than that, he desired to live a worthy life. To do well and make a difference. Yet, and this is the thing that captivates, by the end of the Gospel, *doubting* Thomas was a fully-fledged believer in Jesus and his resurrection. But only *after* taking a good hard look at things for himself.

Following the crucifixion of Jesus, it was reported that he had come back to life. In his Gospel, John records an astonishing conversation Thomas had with the risen Jesus. In looking at this pivotal conversation, I hope to support those who are genuinely unsure of what to make of Jesus and the Christian faith. Those who have reasonable doubt about the wisdom of entering into relationship with him. I don't intend to try to decide the issue for you. Rather, my aim is to present to you the written record of Thomas' interaction with Jesus. To put the issue of his doubts visibly and sharply before you. And in doing so, help you in some small way as you think things through for yourself.

AN APPEARANCE TO SOME

We are told that on the night after Jesus was raised from the dead, he appeared to some of his closest followers. Evidently, they had gathered together in one place and were still not sure what to make of the report of Mary Magdalene (and by now the other women) who claimed to have seen Jesus earlier that same day. They were all together now, that is, all of them except Thomas. He was not there. The text simply reads:

> *Now Thomas, one of the Twelve, called the Twin, was not with them when Jesus came.*

We are not given a reason for what kept Thomas away. He just wasn't there. Absent. A short time later though, even as early as the next day, Thomas did show up. He arrived. And he got the surprise of his life.

> *So the other disciples told him, 'We have seen the Lord.'*

Five one syllable words. Count them. Words that in time would alter the course of human history. Strung together, they ask us to consider an entirely new discovery, a more complete knowledge, a fresh conviction even, that challenges the best of conventional wisdom. Let's be clear: these *witnesses* are advocating for a belief in the bodily resurrection of Jesus. Now, what in the world was Thomas supposed to do with that?

GOOD REASONS FOR DOUBT

He did what any person in their right mind would do. When confronted with news this astounding—a thing that on the face of it defies logic—and which, if proven true, would upend matters long ago considered settled, he simply said:

> *Unless I see in his hands the mark of the nails, and place my finger into the mark of the nails, and place my hand into his side, I will never believe.*

Thomas exercised doubt. In the clearest terms possible. His belief would not go where his eyes, hands and feet could not take him. In exerting doubt, he leveraged the setback of his earlier absence. His doubts would only be assuaged if he had the same experience as the others. He too would have to see Jesus. To touch him for himself. Thomas kept his rational faculties. He retained a measure of reservation. In addition (and this is what I like most), he put his doubts into *words*. He verbalized them. He owned them. In doing so, he may come across as a skeptical soul. But one that we can all admire. So, yes. We are decided. We will not blame Thomas for what he has said. After all, he had his own good reasons. He hadn't seen Jesus for himself.

Did you catch the proofs that Thomas needed? The evidence he considered mandatory? The verification he required?

> *Unless I see… and place my finger… and place my hand… I will never believe.*

These are heavy-duty words. With them, Thomas gives us the properties of real life. Flesh and blood. Hard science. Empirical evidence. All the good stuff. And this is only right. The idea that a man rose from the dead in fulfillment of Old Testament promises is, frankly, incredible. Thomas certainly thought so. The idea that God, in Jesus Christ, provided the world with a risen king, one who saves us from sin and rules us by his word is (from our side of the sun anyway) improbable.

Clearly, this kind of thing isn't to be taken at face value. Is it? No. Not for Thomas anyway. And not for many more like him. Credulity won't do. Most people are like Thomas. They have good reasons for doubt. Therefore, good reasons to think otherwise will have to be provided in return.

Not being there is one of the reasons people have doubts about Jesus and the resurrection and the Christian faith. We were not there. How are we to go about getting around that stubborn fact? We feel our absence places us at a disadvantage. Honestly, a belief in the resurrection far exceeds the level of things that already go by: 'Well, I guess you had to be there to believe it,' or, 'Yes. I swear. I'm telling you the truth. I saw it with my own eyes.' If *being there* is already important for far lesser matters, how can we possibly expect it to be otherwise for something as mind-blowing as the resurrection? We are with Thomas in his provocation. We are eager to see how his conversation with Jesus provides him some resolution. But more than that. We want to understand what it may mean for the doubts we hold close. The ones that endure.

Anyway, at this point in the story, Thomas has laid down his own gauntlet on belief. The other disciples have all heard him. As readers, we fully expect that something will be said to him by one of them. Surely Peter, Andrew, or John will offer a response to Thomas' pronouncement? Where else is Thomas to go with his doubts? But, and this is the interesting thing, it doesn't appear that they had anything to say. Not so much as a single word to persuade. Instead we get days of silence. No meaningful conversation recorded. We are left envisioning them telling him over and over again: 'No, Thomas, really. We have seen the Lord.' Always to be followed with his requirement: 'Unless…'

This stalemate lasted for more than a week. Thomas' reservations, coupled with their obvious frustrations, brought their discussions to a standstill. Completely motionless. Their experience stood in stark contrast to his own. I suppose the only questions now were: 'How long can this impasse go on?' and 'What will break the deadlock?' Everyone waited. Until, out of nowhere, a miracle occurred. One that I trust will help you with your own needs and requirements for belief.

DOUBTS ARE DISTURBED

John's Gospel continues:

> *Eight days later, his disciples were inside again, and Thomas was with them. Although the doors were locked, Jesus*

came and stood among them and said,
'Peace be with you.'

This time, Thomas was there. He was on the other side of the door. He was present and accounted for. I find the gloss about the doors being *locked* an interesting detail. This same thing was mentioned by John earlier, in reference to Jesus' previous appearance. There, we were told that the doors had been locked from *the inside*. What are we to make of this?

First, it is good to know that the first followers of Jesus weren't foolish. Even after eight days, they had their heads on straight. With their leader so recently killed, and the city still in a state of confusion, who can blame them for wondering what might happen if some officials came knocking? Put simply, gaining entrance to the room was not going to occur haphazardly. It would require an unasked-for intrusion. A disturbance. The very thing Jesus is said to have accomplished. The Gospel indicates that he was suddenly standing in their midst. What are we to make of this?

Let us take this from it: Thomas' doubts were going to be assuaged in the only way they could be—through the physical reality of the resurrection. Suddenly, Jesus was just there, standing in their midst. No door needed. Thomas was faced directly, disconcertingly even, by a miraculous appearance of Jesus. In other words, the thing that helped Thomas get over the hump was that he got to see Jesus for himself. It is as though Thomas had to wait for his time to come.

Now, I know what you are thinking. This is all well and good for Thomas, but I am not sure how it can possibly be of any help to us. Now our question has evolved. 'What is the relationship between Thomas' *seeing* and my *believing*? What is the link in the chain between him and me—between what helped him and what can help me?' But, no sooner are the questions out of our mouth than John's

Gospel presses on. The narrative travels. And not toward us. But toward Jesus and Thomas, now both in the same room. The time for *their* exchange on doubt has come. Our questions will have to wait.

DOUBTS ARE ADDRESSED

The one who initiates the conversation is Jesus. And his opening line surprises: 'Peace be with you.' In the original language, *you* is plural in form. It is spoken to *everyone* in the room, including Thomas. We didn't expect this. Why is this the first thing Jesus said? What did he mean by it? And what might Thomas, or any of us who have resurrection doubts stand to gain by it?

Well, *peace to you* could be the right first words simply because they counter the shock of the sudden appearance of Jesus. He disturbed the peace in the first place. Perhaps he is now trying to restore some. This is a possible reading of the text. A statement to soften the shock. If so, it is an *affirmation* of sorts. Nothing more. *Peace to you* reveals a solid attempt to mollify their fears.

That said, the ambiguity of the line might also hint at something more. Is Jesus only trying to calm their hearts? Or, is he making a declaration that will only be understood later? Let me explain. Earlier in John's Gospel, Jesus promised to leave his *peace* with them. By it, he meant the presence of the Holy Spirit. Does he intend the same thing here? Is this a *pronouncement* of that peace? A statement that victory has been won? Death has been defeated? And that *peace* can be had? Is the Holy Spirit now theirs? If so, then the first words Thomas hears from the mouth of Jesus do more than create space for him. With these words, Jesus is placing his own stamp of approval on the disciples. This is no ordinary peace.

Knowing this can be useful to us. It gives us something to consider. Perhaps Jesus intends for Thomas to understand his resurrection as the reasonable outcome and fulfillment of promises God made to Israel. Promises that prophets set down in writing long ago. Think of it as the consequence of God's personal guarantee about a *peace* brokered by his only Son. Is that what is going on here? Is Jesus telling us that the enmity that once existed between God and humanity has been put to *rest* by his own death and resurrection? Peace does convey the idea of rest, the cessation of hostilities.

I know. This is a lot to take in. And I won't press the possibility further. But, if this is what Jesus meant by *peace to you,* then the body of evidence available to us, the data revealed to support us through doubt, just got bigger. We find help for our doubt from the complete story line and unified testimony of the Old Testament. Wow. Imagine it. The *peace* that Jesus might one day pronounce on *you* could be connected to the promises he fulfilled. This has all been recorded for us in in the Old

Testament. And we are free to examine it at any time.

DOUBTS ARE REBUKED

We can be sure that on the night Jesus pronounced this blessing upon them, no one in the room had any time for this kind of reflection. That would have to come later, both for them and for you. The narrative is again on the move. Jesus is ready to do more than address Thomas' doubts by his presence. He is going to deliver some hard-hitting direct speech of his own. Take a look.

> Then he said to Thomas, 'Put your finger here, and see my hands; and put out your hand, and place it in my side. Do not disbelieve but believe.'

There is a saying: 'Be careful what you wish for.' Applied here, it looks like Thomas got more than he bargained for. Do you remember his first words on the matter of resurrection doubt? Jesus' words here mirror them. When told by the others that Jesus was alive, Thomas had said, 'Unless I see in his hands the mark of the nails, and place my finger into the mark of the nails, and place my hand into his side, I will never believe.' It seems as though Jesus overheard him when he said it! The impact of this had to be big. Seriously. We have Jesus looking Thomas in the eye and saying, 'Well, have a look at it, young man. Put your finger here… place your hand there.'

It reads like an open *rebuke*. That much is clear. There is no other way around it. Jesus was not a fan of Thomas and his doubt. And this should give us pause. Does Jesus disagree with our opening statement that doubt is a virtue? An asset? Worse yet, does he think it shameful? Unwanted in his world? Like some disagreeable commodity? And if he does, do we really want to align ourselves with him? To what end? To a charade of getting in line behind a man and his religion?

Or, are we missing something? Is there another way to understand this? Yes. There is. Thomas should have been more willing than he was to accept the testimony of his friends. He could have trusted them. Their evidence should have counted for something. That is what Jesus is telling him. That is the takeaway. Thomas knew them. And he knew them well. But, in this most important of all instances, he chose to dig in his heels. For Thomas, at least, the evidence presented should have resulted in something other than his stubborn insistence on having to be an eyewitness. Clearly, Thomas could have—I suppose Jesus is saying even more, *Thomas should have*—come to a place of belief, not doubt, on the basis of what his friends had told him.

Perhaps there is something here for us to consider? Must Jesus appear before us in bodily form for us to believe? Does he have to show up in our living room, sometime after we have already locked up for the night? I hope not. It feels like it would be the height of arrogance to demand it. We don't demand that kind of confirmation for any other belief. And so, we have run into another help on doubt (beyond the record of the Old Testament already mentioned). We should place more stock in trusted friends, colleagues, and neighbors who have looked into the matter and come out believing. Certainly they can bear *some* of the weight of certainty on our behalf.

DOUBT AND THE MATTER OF DISBELIEF

For Thomas, the stakes for his ongoing doubt are about to get higher. If Jesus' soft rebuke wasn't enough, he now says: 'Do not disbelieve, but believe.' Looking closely at the grammar, these words convey two sides of a command. You should think of them as two orders. One is stated in the negative. The other, in the positive. I can paraphrase them this way: 'Thomas, stop disbelieving and start believing. And do it now!' Jesus sure has a way of putting things. It makes me wonder whether Thomas should have been called *Disbelieving* Thomas.

What are we to make of this escalation of the pressure on Thomas. Is this fair? Does Jesus think that to doubt is to disbelieve? As though they are one and the same thing? More personally, can we not have doubts about Jesus and his resurrection without being reprimanded like this? Or, according to Jesus, do my doubts cast me beyond the pale of divine acceptability?

Surely, not all doubt can be equated with disbelief. That would be going too far. But how to know when we've crossed the line?

For us, this is the hard part. We are so accustomed to speaking of the advantages of doubt, we forget its dangers. Over time, doubt grows into firm disbelief. How does that evolution happen? For Thomas, remaining in doubt after being confronted with the good and credible eyewitness testimony of friends was the problem. For us, it can occur when we set aside rational arguments, good research, and reasonable solutions.

If we are honest with ourselves, we have all done it. We have reasons for not wanting to believe things. Predispositions that need protecting. Biases that need covering. Behavior that craves its continuance. Is it possible that, if we met Jesus, he might confront us on some of our doubts? Would he call me out? And then call me to something else?

These are difficult questions. They require care, wisdom, and a bit of personal self-reflection. However, we can say this: Jesus came down hard on Thomas because his doubts were nothing short of disbelief. *For him,* the feigning of doubt was a cover, a shield, a way of hiding behind his abject unbelief. And I guess we should have seen this coming. After all, the last words he spoke in defense of his doubt were actually '… *I will not believe.*'

We can only surmise how Jesus knew this about Thomas. Was it because he knew him so well? The text doesn't tell us. However, what we do know is this: Jesus called out his dishonesty. His artificiality. His disingenuousness. Don't let that happen to you. Don't live in a state of self-deception. It's not worth it. If Thomas' disbelief characterizes you to this point in your life, then own it. I'm not sure how any of us move forward without doing at least that. Perhaps this is an additional takeaway for us. It is better to become a person of belief or disbelief, than the person Thomas had become: duplicitous in his self-congratulatory doubt.

DECLARATION REPLACES DOUBT

A lot has transpired for Thomas in a short period of time. Think of it. So many things. Jesus' *'peace to you'* introduced the possibility that Old Testament promises had been fulfilled, and as such, that a storehouse of evidence for the resurrection was available to support him.

But there was more. Thomas had learned the importance of being open to the testimony of his friends. Their words should have received more weight than he had given them. He should have known that he wasn't in this thing all by himself. Beyond these things, he was also lovingly called out on his disbelief, something to keep him from wandering further into a life of lies and self-deception. All these things were helpful to him, I am sure. And to us.

We could say more. But, we have arrived at a moment in the conversation where Thomas says something that (for me anyway), appears to be as abrupt as Jesus' earlier entrance into the room. Thomas embraced faith. Disbelief gave way. And from right where he stood. He didn't even need to walk across the room to put his fingers into the nail holes of Jesus' hands. He didn't have to. The text simply reads:

Thomas answered him, 'My Lord and my God!'

Wow. This is Thomas' life transforming moment, and in his own words. His confession of faith. His own declaration. Think of them as his doorway through doubt. Put differently, they are his own joyful discovery of something new. His own arriving at a more complete understanding of our world, the way it works—and most importantly, to what end. In other words, Thomas came to believe, to affirm what he would call *real* things, better things, things that can be proven, trusted, and rationally called true.

We should pause on his profession of faith. Notice that his declaration, beyond doubt, has *two* parts. He calls Jesus both 'my Lord' *and* 'my God.' This is interesting. Taken together, Thomas now believes Jesus to be the altogether righteous man. Unlike any other. Worthy to be followed, and of Thomas' complete allegiance. Thus, *my Lord*. But also, he asserts that Jesus is mysteriously greater even than that. *My God*. This is Christianity's classic formulation concerning Jesus. Fully human. Fully divine. Son of David. And Son of God.

In short, Thomas is now a follower *and* worshiper of Jesus. He believes *this* Jesus fulfilled the ancient promises to Israel. He was God descended into flesh and blood. With the resurrection proving it so. To put it bluntly, for Thomas, Jesus is all that really matters.

DOUBT AND OUR OWN NEED FOR DISCOVERY

This is all good for Thomas. We are even happy for him. But what about us? Where do we come in? How can we possibly enter through that same door? What will turn the key that unlocks our doubt? Beyond, of course, the help we have already gleaned from Thomas' encounter, the message and evidence from the Old Testament, giving some weight to the testimony of others, and the admonition to evaluate if our doubts are actually disbelief?

At the end of the day, we still don't have the advantage of Jesus' appearance. We didn't get to hear the sound of his voice or experience the jarring reality of his bodily presence. So, we are back to the questions we posed at first, 'What is the relationship between Thomas' *seeing* and my *believing*? What is the link in the chain that helped him and how can it help me?'

Well, for starters, take heart. Jesus' conversation with Thomas isn't over. There is more to come. In addition, we need to let John (the one who recorded this conversation) have his say on the matter. After all, he wrote with an aim to assist us, his readers, well aware that we could not be advantaged in the way he was.

JESUS: HOPE FOR OUR DOUBTS

First, let's look at the words of Jesus. What does he say in response to Thomas' confession of faith? Is there anything in it for us?

Jesus said to him, 'Have you believed because you have seen me? Blessed are those who have not seen and yet have believed.'

Here we find a first glimmer of hope. While Jesus is glad that Thomas believes, his question pushes beyond a celebration of that fact. Instead, Jesus brings us under the sound of his voice. Did you notice? His final words in the conversation are directed toward us, *we* are in the room. *We* are the intended audience sitting under the sound of his voice. And this is what we heard him say: A blessing (a benediction of sorts), a stamp of approval rests on everyone who will come to believe in him without ever having seen him. Here it is again:

Blessed are those who have not seen and yet have believed.

This is important news and very useful to us. The meaning is this: Jesus fully expects that people who were *not there* will nevertheless be capable of believing in him. And more. A blessing awaits all who do. This is great! Promising. And like nothing we have read yet. That said, it does raise a question: On what grounds? How is this promising expectation accomplished? What must happen for Jesus to make good on his blessing?

JOHN: HELP FOR OUR DOUBTS

If someone could begin to sketch out an approach on this question, someone who was there at the time, we should have enough of 'the good stuff' to decide the matter. So, who else was there?

Interestingly, from here on, it will be John's voice that we hear. What does he say? Does he provide a way forward? Can he guide us? I mean, he should, right? The answer to these questions is *yes*. John does. His next words are these:

Now Jesus did many other signs in the presence of his disciples, which are not written in this book; but these are written so that you may believe that Jesus is the Christ, the Son of God, and that by believing you may have life in his name.

This is enlightening. The final words of Jesus, which include us, are followed by John's words which are designed to help us. A doorway is made. A key is given. An idea is advanced that, if embraced, will assist us in deciding on doubt. Here it is.

…but these are written so that you may believe that Jesus is the Christ, the Son of God, and that by believing you may have life in his name.

The *these* John is referring to are all the events he has *written* down in his Gospel (including the conversation between Jesus and Thomas).

Putting this together, John is asking us to consider the link between Thomas' *seeing* and our *believing* to be his own *writing*. In other words, he is making an argument that your walk from doubt to faith can be made from right where you are, by trusting in the veracity of what he has written down.

Ironically, the idea isn't all that far-fetched. And for a number of reasons. First, the author of this Gospel is thought to be John, an *eyewitness* to the events in question. For certain, someone had to be there. Someone had to vouch for it. To believe without a witness would be foolish. The claims are just too great. But, to disbelieve John's witness may be equally foolish. Let me explain: We are wrong to think that *seeing is believing*, if by it we mean that only those present at an event can be expected to hold it to be true. That's just not the way life works. In anything. We believe in a host of things on the basis of eyewitness testimony.

Second, *reading is often the source of that believing*. Should the standard be any different just because we are considering

Jesus? This demand for *seeing*, rather than *reading,* raises the bar too high. Truth be told, we prefer to have things in writing. Why? Because when a person puts their name on something, a binding takes place. Words written secure something real. Credibility. In a court of law, it is more often than not the testimony of *words on paper* that is considered conclusive.

The same is true in other arenas of life. Think about it. You and I probably give some credence to a newspaper account of an event that occurred yesterday on the other side of the world. Even though we were not there. Why? Because the reporter's written record is something we take seriously. That is all John is asking for. Knowing this to be the case, continuing in a state of doubt about the resurrection of Jesus will be more difficult for us now. We must either believe what John has written or disbelieve him. There isn't a lot of middle ground. Were we to meet him on the street, I think he would press us toward one decision or the other. For him this is personal. He believes.

Coming to grips with the fact that *reading is believing* can be a great help to us on doubt. A 19th century preacher put it this way:

> *I reckon that many of you in business are quite content to get written orders for goods, and when you don't, you do not require a purchaser to ask you in person; you would just as soon he should not: In fact, you commonly say you would rather have it in black and white, is it not so? Well then, you have your wish, here is the call in black and white.*[3]

Never underestimate the significance of what God's Word reveals to you in black and white.

WHAT TO DO NOW?

From here, it is all on you. I can't decide for you. So, what do you want to do now?

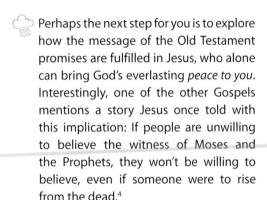 Perhaps the next step for you is to explore how the message of the Old Testament promises are fulfilled in Jesus, who alone can bring God's everlasting *peace to you*. Interestingly, one of the other Gospels mentions a story Jesus once told with this implication: If people are unwilling to believe the witness of Moses and the Prophets, they won't be willing to believe, even if someone were to rise from the dead.[4]

Or, maybe it's time for you to speak with a friend or family member or another credible person you know who already believes. After all, we have already seen that others can be trusted to bear some of the weight for us.

That said, this short book may help you to live more honestly. Not to hide behind the word *doubt*, if that is not where you are. However, given the stakes, I hope you will think long and hard before becoming a person of disbelief.

 For others, I hope the conversation between Thomas and Jesus helped you arrive at your own life-transforming moment. At faith. Belief. To a day you will long remember. In reading God's Word, I hope some of you ended up meeting Jesus.

Believe me, this last possibility is still happening. Everyday. To both women and men from all over the world. Allow me to close with a true story. A student, studying science, entered school as an agnostic. He did not know if God existed. But he went along one night to listen to a preacher explain the gospel message. A Bible reading was given and an explanation followed. And at the end of it, this student believed. Later, he captured the event in his own words, words written down:

As for the former agnostic, who a few minutes later was running back to his lodgings to be in by midnight, 'it was as though my feet scarcely touched the ground, and I have the most vivid recollection of saying to myself over and over, as I ran, "I've seen Jesus! I've seen Jesus!"—words that I had certainly never used before, nor heard anyone else use.'[5]

If this person's experience resonates with yours, simply tell God so. Tell him that you believe. That you take John at his word. And like Thomas, that you have faith in Jesus—you are willing to call him your Lord and your God.

If that is your decision, I also want to encourage you to find a church that teaches these things. They can help you grow.

JOHN 20:24-31

24 Now Thomas, one of the twelve, called the Twin, was not with them when Jesus came. 25 So the other disciples told him, 'We have seen the Lord.' But he said to them, 'Unless I see in his hands the mark of the nails, and place my finger into the mark of the nails, and place my hand into his side, I will never believe.' 26 Eight days later, his disciples were inside again, and Thomas was with them. Although the doors were locked, Jesus came and stood among them and said, 'Peace be with you.' 27 Then he said to Thomas, 'Put your finger here, and see my hands; and put out your hand, and place it in my side. Do not disbelieve, but believe.' 28 Thomas answered him, 'My Lord and my God!' 29 Jesus said to him, 'Have you believed because you have seen me? Blessed are those who have not seen and yet have believed.' 30 Now Jesus did many other signs in the presence of the disciples, which are not written in this book; 31 but these are written so that you may believe that Jesus is the Christ, the Son of God, and that by believing you may have life in his name.

ENDNOTES

1. Leo Tolstoy, *Anna Karenina* (trans. L. Maude and A. Maude; Mineola, NY: Dover, 1885), 396.

2. This man's encounter with Jesus can be found in full by reading John 20:24-31. I encourage you to read it. The text can be found on page 53. Unless otherwise marked, all subsequent quotations are from this passage.

3. C. H. Spurgeon, 'Abraham's Prompt Obedience to the Call of God' (1242), in *The Spurgeon Archive*. http://archive. spurgeon.org/sermons/1242.php. Accessed September 20, 2018.

4. Luke 16:19-31.

5. John Charles Pollock, *A Cambridge Movement*, (London: Murray, 1953), 212.

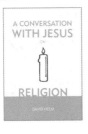
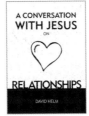

WITH **JESUS** SERIES

**A CONVERSATION
WITH JESUS ON
TRUTH**
9781527103276

**A CONVERSATION
WITH JESUS ON
HOPE**
9781527103290

**A CONVERSATION
WITH JESUS ON...
BOXSET**
9781527103238

To:

Bro: Joe

From:

_____

Date:

9/18/15

BIBLE TAILS™

The Little Book of

HEAVENLY HUMOR

By Jon Huckeby & Nicholas DeYoung

HARVEST HOUSE PUBLISHERS

EUGENE, OREGON

The Little Book of Heavenly Humor
Copyright © 2011 by DaySpring Cards.
Used under license. All rights reserved.

Published by Harvest House Publishers
Eugene, Oregon 97402
www.harvesthousepublishers.com

ISBN 978-0-7369-4739-8

Design and production by
Harvest House Publishers, Eugene, Oregon

All Scripture quotations, unless otherwise indicated, are taken from The Holy Bible, *New International Version® NIV®*. Copyright © 1973, 1978, 1984, 2011 by Biblica, Inc.™ Used by permission. All rights reserved worldwide. Verses marked TLB are taken from *The Living Bible*, Copyright © 1971. Used by permission of Tyndale House Publishers, Inc., Wheaton, IL 60189 USA. All rights reserved. Verses marked KJV are taken from the King James Version of the Bible.

Printed in China
12 13 14 15 16 17 18 / LP / 10 9 8 7 6 5 4 3 2 1

ASKING GOD TO BLESS YOU WITH MULTIPLIED JOY TODAY.

For some on the ark, it felt more like 80 days and 80 nights.

DO NOT FEAR,
FOR I AM WITH YOU...
I AM YOUR GOD.
ISAIAH 41:10

AWARDS NIGHT ON THE ARK

BE BEAUTIFUL INSIDE, IN YOUR HEARTS, WITH THE LASTING CHARM OF A GENTLE AND QUIET SPIRIT THAT IS SO PRECIOUS TO GOD.

1 PETER 3:4 TLB

BABY MOSES

SHE GOT A PAPYRUS BASKET... PLACED THE CHILD IN IT AND PUT IT AMONG THE REEDS ALONG THE BANK OF THE NILE.

EXODUS 2:3

BALAAM'S DONKEY

THEN THE LORD CAUSED THE DONKEY TO SPEAK!

NUMBERS 22:28 TLB

BATHROOMS ON THE ARK

TWO BY TWO THEY CAME, MALE AND FEMALE, JUST AS GOD HAD COMMANDED.

THEN THE LORD GOD CLOSED THE DOOR AND SHUT THEM IN.

GENESIS 7:16 TLB

PREPARING FOR
THE EYE OF THE NEEDLE

BUMPER STICKERS 35 A.D.

HOW'S MY GALLOP?
CALL 800·555-1234

PILATE·HEROD
VOTE A.D. 25

My other Donkey
is a horse.

Bray if you love Jesus!

THE COLT WAS BROUGHT TO JESUS...
FOR HIM TO RIDE ON.

MARK 11:7 TLB

THERE THE ANGEL OF THE LORD APPEARED TO HIM IN FLAMES OF FIRE FROM WITHIN A BUSH.

EXODUS 3:2

The original OneStar Navigation System

AFTER THEY HAD HEARD THE KING,
THEY WENT ON THEIR WAY, AND
THE STAR THEY HAD SEEN WHEN IT
ROSE WENT AHEAD OF THEM UNTIL
IT STOPPED OVER THE PLACE
WHERE THE CHILD WAS.

MATTHEW 2:9

CAMEL PARKING
$3 / HR

THEN THE LORD GOD ASKED THE WOMAN,
"HOW COULD YOU
DO SUCH A THING?"

"THE SERPENT TRICKED ME,"
SHE REPLIED.

GENESIS 3:13 TLB

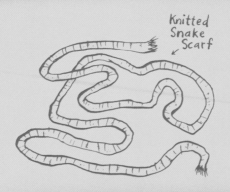

Knitted
Snake
Scarf

THE DOVE CAME IN TO HIM IN THE EVENING; AND, LO, IN HER MOUTH WAS AN OLIVE LEAF.

GENESIS 8:11 KJV

THEY SAW
JESUS
APPROACHING
THE BOAT,
WALKING ON
THE WATER.

JOHN 6:19

I dare you to go nibble on his toes.

Pharaoh's Dog

BE GLAD AND REJOICE...
BE HAPPY AND JOYFUL.

PSALM 68:3

HE TOUCHED THEIR EYES
AND...THEIR SIGHT
WAS RESTORED.

MATTHEW 9:29-30

WILL WORK
FOR
DOG FOOD

AND THE PIG, THOUGH IT HAS A DIVIDED HOOF, DOES NOT CHEW THE CUD: IT IS UNCLEAN FOR YOU.

YOU MUST NOT EAT THEIR MEAT.

LEVITICUS 11:7-8

'THIS SON OF MINE WAS... LOST AND IS FOUND." SO THE PARTY BEGAN.

LUKE 15:24 TLB

Herman catches a break.

THE ISRAELITES WENT THROUGH THE SEA ON DRY GROUND, WITH A WALL OF WATER ON THEIR RIGHT AND ON THEIR LEFT.

EXODUS 14:22

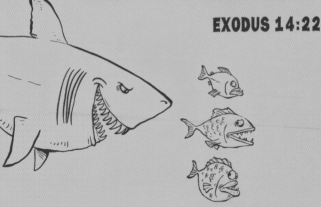

THE LION'S DEN

THEN THE KING COMMANDED, AND THEY BROUGHT DANIEL, AND CAST HIM INTO THE DEN OF LIONS.

DANIEL 6:16 KJV

GIVE THANKS TO THE LORD, FOR HE IS GOOD.

PSALM 118:29

IT WAS OBVIOUS BY THE END OF THE DAY THAT ADAM WAS RUNNING OUT OF GOOD NAMES.

THE WHALE THAT SWALLOWED JONAH

JONAH WAS IN THE BELLY OF THE FISH THREE DAYS AND THREE NIGHTS.

JONAH 1:17 KJV

DON'T HIDE YOUR LIGHT! LET IT SHINE FOR ALL.

MATTHEW 5:15 TLB

BIBLE TRIVIA

BAT

CHAMELEON

ELEPHANT

UNICORN

WHICH ONE OF THESE ANIMALS IS <u>NOT</u> MENTIONED
IN THE BIBLE?

THESE ARE THEY OF WHICH YE SHALL NOT EAT...THE BAT.

DEUTERONOMY 14:12,18 KJV

THESE ALSO SHALL BE UNCLEAN UNTO YOU... THE CHAMELEON.

LEVITICUS 11:29-30 KJV

HE HATH AS IT WERE THE STRENGTH OF AN UNICORN.

NUMBERS 23:22 KJV

SO DON'T WORRY AT ALL ABOUT HAVING ENOUGH FOOD.

MATTHEW 6:31 TLB

THE BETHLEHEM MANGER